The Women in Blue Helmets

The publisher gratefully acknowledges the generous support of the Director's Circle of the University of California Press Foundation, whose members are:

Harriett & Richard Gold
Thomas & Barbara Metcalf
Jerome Moss
Nancy & Roger Boas
Barbara Z. Otto
Marilyn Lee & Harvey Schneider
John & Jo De Luca
Gary & Cary Hart
Lloyd Cotsen
Byron Georgiou & Dr. Therese Collins
Dana Baldwin
Barbara L. Ayers
Emerson Reis
Margaret L. Pillsbury
John Winthrop Haeger
Ajay Shah & Lata Krishnan

The Women in Blue Helmets

GENDER, POLICING, AND THE UN'S FIRST
ALL-FEMALE PEACEKEEPING UNIT

Lesley J. Pruitt

UNIVERSITY OF CALIFORNIA PRESS

University of California Press, one of the most distinguished university presses in the United States, enriches lives around the world by advancing scholarship in the humanities, social sciences, and natural sciences. Its activities are supported by the UC Press Foundation and by philanthropic contributions from individuals and institutions. For more information, visit www.ucpress.edu.

University of California Press
Oakland, California

Library of Congress Cataloging-in-Publication Data

Names: Pruitt, Lesley J., author.
Title: The women in blue helmets : gender, policing, and the UN's first all-female peacekeeping unit / Lesley J. Pruitt.
Description: Oakland, California : University of California Press, [2016] | "2016 | Includes bibliographical references and index.
Identifiers: LCCN 2016005857 (print) | LCCN 2016007189 (ebook) | ISBN 9780520290600 (cloth) | ISBN 9780520290617 (pbk.) | ISBN 9780520964716 (Epub)
Subject: LCSH: Women and peace. | Policewomen. | United Nations—Peacekeeping forces. | United Nation. Security Council. Resolution 1325. | International police.
Classification: LCC JZ5578. P78 2016 (print) | LCC JZ5578 (ebook) | DDC 355.3/57—dc23
LC record available at http://lccn.loc.gov/2016005857

25 24 23 22 21 20 19 18 17 16
10 9 8 7 6 5 4 3 2 1

Contents

Acknowledgments

A University of Melbourne Arts Faculty Research Development Grant provided funding for the fieldwork necessary to complete this project. RMIT University supported me during revisions of the manuscript and provided funding for indexing.

Chapters 4 and 6 include modified versions of some portions of the following articles: "All-Female Police Contingents: Feminism and the Discourse of Armed Protection," *International Peacekeeping* 20, no. 1 (2013): 67–79; and "Looking Back, Moving Forward: The Role of the International Community in Addressing Conflict-Related Sexual Violence," *Journal of Women, Politics and Policy* 33, no. 4 (2012): 299–321. I thank the editors of those journals and the anonymous reviewers of those articles for their feedback.

I have benefited extensively from the generosity of a number of friends and colleagues who have provided editorial advice, guidance, and support in various aspects of this research project. They include Chris Agius, Kevin Arruch, Helen Berents, Roland, Bleiker, Mark Chou, David Davis, Shannon Drysdale Walsh, Constance Duncombe, Michelle Dunn, Nicole George, Laura Huber, Natalie Hudson, Charlie Hunt, Erica Rose Jeffrey, Katrina Lee-Koo, Ross Marlay, Laura McLeod, Sara Meger, Swati Parashar, Avery

Dorothy Howard Poole, Leah Ruppanner, Laura Shepherd, Sarah Teitt, Ann Tickner, and Jacqui True.

I am also grateful to the University of California Press team and the anonymous reviewers who responded to this manuscript. They have provided constructive, thoughtful feedback, which I hope has been well incorporated here. Any and all errors that remain are my own.

Abbreviations

AWPS	All-women police station
AWPU	All-women police unit
CRPF	Central Reserve Police Force
DM	*Delegacia da muljer* [all-women police station in Brazil]
DPKO	Department of Peacekeeping Operations
FFPU	All-female formed police unit
FPU	Formed police unit
IPS	Indian Police Service
MARWOPNET	Mano River Women's Peace Network
UN	United Nations
UNMIL	United Nations Mission in Liberia
UNPOL	United Nations Police Division
WIPNET	Women in Peacebuilding Network
WPS agenda	Women, Peace and Security agenda

Introduction

You need to see how things begin in order to understand what they become.

In January 2007, the first all-female formed police unit (FFPU) was deployed in United Nations (UN) peacekeeping. Indian media headlines reported, "The Ladies from India Have Landed in Liberia" and hailed the initiative, declaring the "Battalion a Hit in Liberia."[1] The contingent consisted of 105 women peacekeepers recruited from across India's Central Reserve Police Force, a paramilitary police organization. The first group was deemed a success by the UN and media reports, and a rotation system was put in place so that the contingent would be replaced annually. This means that an FFPU has been deployed in Liberia nine times by this book's publication.

The first commander of the FFPU, Seema Dhundia, said of her team, "These girls are experienced and have been trained. They have worked in areas of India where there was insurgency. They will do a good job and the Liberian ladies will get motivated and inspired to come forward and join the regular police."[2] She may well have been right: since the FFPU's introduction, Liberia has seen a significant increase in women joining the national police, and the UN Mission in Liberia now has a higher proportion of women in its police forces than any other UN peacekeeping mission, at 16.67 percent compared to 8.2 percent in UN policing overall.[3] Two other FFPUs have since been deployed from Bangladesh to Haiti and

Democratic Republic of the Congo,[4] but little public information is yet available on those deployments. This book focuses on the Indian contingent as the first and longest-standing FFPU.

FFPUs represent an approach to bringing women into peacekeeping that provides an alternative to mixed-gender, male-majority units. Instead of expecting individual women to adapt themselves to the existing male-dominated system, FPPUs provide the option of all-female spaces and pursue structural and procedural changes that give serious attention to women's needs and motivations. While this approach is not perfect and does not perfectly meet the UN's stated goal of having women and men work side by side to achieve peace and security, it is a timely measure that pragmatically pursues long-term goals while working with available short-term options. In doing so, FFPUs may enhance security for women and men here and now. In fact, it seems they have. President Ellen Johnson Sirleaf of Liberia was so impressed by their performance that she personally requested that they provide her security detail, a security job that has been traditionally male. As the former FFPU coordinator for Liberia told me, "They were proven in a riot in a deadly situation. They don't flinch. That caught the eye of President Sirleaf. When her mansion caught on fire they stepped up to provide security in the adjacent building. She was so happy they were female, professional, and doing, what did she say? 'A bang up job!'"

In telling the story of this first FFPU from India, this book explores how the introduction of the initial FFPU to Liberia increases the participation of women and directly challenges gender norms that suggest women are unsuited to security work. At the same time, some nuance is needed to avoid viewing women instrumentally as "resources" who can "naturally" reach other women in postconflict zones where they are deployed. The research conducted for this project suggests that in many instances women probably can better reach women; however, this is not "natural." It is more likely due to women's mistrust of men because of gendered violence, women's experience-based understanding of the harm of gendered stereotypes applied to women, and women making an effort to *learn* how to help victims—something that men working in peace and security roles should certainly also be expected to do. Meanwhile, participation in FFPUs may offer the women who participate in them significant leadership opportunities and relevant security experience that may be used in later FFPUs but also in mixed-gender contingents, which remain the majority of contingents in UN peacekeeping. With peacekeeping operations continuously requesting more formed police units and individual police officers, finding effective ways of recruiting more police, both women and men, to peacekeeping will be crucial.

Given that the vast majority of women who have participated as police peacekeepers have done so through mixed-gender contingents, to date most scholarship on women and peacekeeping has addressed that arena. As the first book-length analysis of an FFPU, this book builds on existing scholarship and takes it in new directions. Over the years, much of the scholarship on women's roles in peacekeeping has evidenced cynicism about what women's participation might mean for peace and security.[5] Indeed, many may be critical of the capacity of women to be a source of positive change, for various social, structural, and professional reasons.[6] Efforts at including women may thus be seen as tokenistic, empty gestures that are additive as opposed to transformative. However, as discussed in detail later, some of these charges may be specifically related to adding women into existing male-dominated units or spaces, rather than to inherent problems that would arise no matter where and how women took part in peacekeeping. Recognizing the important contributions of these critical efforts, the feminist critique offered here interrogates essentialized assumptions (e.g., that women are better protectors of women because they are inherently and universally less intimidating, more sensitive, and better at dealing with sexual violence cases). At the same time, this book explicitly seeks to uncover opportunities and potential for positive change through a nuanced analysis and deep engagement with a rich set of data that has yet to be explored.

BACKGROUND ON THE RESEARCH

My interest in this topic comes from a problem-driven approach to research in general and a feminist approach to theory and methods. This framework foregrounds all work that I do, as feminists argue that *"the questions that are asked—*or more important, *those that are not asked—*are as determinative of the adequacy of the project as any answers that we can discover."[7] Hence, I take an explicitly normative approach in disclosing that, like many feminist scholars, I believe that institutional and grassroots approaches to peace and security *ought* to better account for, incorporate, respond to, and support women and girls in order to create a better and more peaceful world for everyone. I therefore consider a broad range of questions that have led to my interest in the FFPU, such as those posed by Kimberly Theidon and Kelly Phenice: "How could women be incorporated most effectively into existing international systems? What kinds of policies or models of intervention would ensure a genuine, comprehensive, and thorough response to women's concerns? What should be included among women's issues during conflict and postconflict periods? Are there ways to ensure that the global agenda reflects the local and regional priorities of socially, culturally, and historically situated women?"[8]

These broader questions inform the specific questions behind this book:

(1) How did the FFPU come about?

(2) What made it possible?

(3) What was expected from it?

(4) What has come from it?

(5) What can the story of the FFPU tell us more broadly about international approaches to gender equity, peace, and security?

Studying the FFPU is important, since, although literature on women in peacekeeping exists, no systematic studies have been done on women in formed police units.[9] Likewise, examining the introduction of FFPUs contributes to filling in missing pieces of this research puzzle by looking at whether and how FFPUs might operate differently or be perceived differently from all-male or mixed-gender contingents. Although this study focuses on women-staffed units, and through that considers gendered patterns of understanding, the intent is not to conflate gender with women, as doing so can limit "the transformative potential of endeavors in the research, policy or practitioner arenas."[10] Instead, I employ a feminist approach to observe inequalities and differences between men and women while conducting a study that rejects views situating women as victims, as inherently peaceful, or as destined for solely domestic duties. In doing so, this book follows critical, constructivist feminist international relations scholars, who explain gender as being "first, fundamentally social; second, an expression of power; and third, an organizing principle' for war specifically, and politics more generally . . . and set out to study it *empirically* (or as it exists in global politics) and to criticize its *normative impact* (characterizing gender subordination as ethically wrong)."[11]

J. Ann Tickner, in line with the *American Heritage Dictionary*, defines *empirical* as "guided by practical experience and not theory," distinguishing it from *empiricism*, defined as "employment of empirical methods in science."[12] Likewise, feminist empirical research has often been situated in critical, constructivist frameworks like the one adopted here.[13] It includes examination of the gender dynamics of institutions as part of the development of theory, noting that "theory is always for someone and for some purpose," and follows critical theory because it "stands apart from the prevailing order of the world and asks how that order came about."[14] Doing so makes it possible to guide strategic action to enact an alternative order,[15] one that is more peaceful in traditional terms and more inclusive of women and that explores possibilities for both gender subordination and challenges to it. The empirical feminist research pursued in this book includes looking at how women in Liberia and India perceive and relate to the FFPU, how the women deployed in the FFPU may or may not benefit from their participation in the FFPU, and how key actors in related institutions situate FFPUs as a policy and as a practice.

As most of the scholarly work on peacekeepers to date has focused on men in peacekeeping, this book develops our understandings to include women, but it has other important functions. The presence of women in peacekeeping can render masculine norms and gender visible in practice, exposing inadequacies and biases of existing peacekeeping practice and possibly "paving the way for real change."[16] Women's participation also has significant implications for deconstructing the notion that security work could be seen as gender neutral. Police organizations are not and never have been gender neutral, so it is necessary to uncover the extent to which policing must be coded as masculine in gender to be legitimate or effective.[17] Moreover, when it comes to theory, "Taking women seriously always has the effect of enabling us to see men as men. That is, when all men are treated as if they matter, those men appear to be generals, authorities, activists, police, farmers, soldiers, managers, investors, economists, writers, and insurgents. That serves to hide their masculinities."[18]

As socially constructed gender hierarchies function to privilege men and masculinity, including in the peace and security field, feminist scholars seek "to postulate a world that could be otherwise."[19] Part of doing that means seeking out different experiences and voices that diverge from the norm of hegemonic masculinity. After all, "Reports from some views can open critical sight lines blocked from some others, and can help to reveal how some views hide others."[20] Thus I have especially sought to uncover how the introduction and implementation of the FFPU reveal gender biases in institutions, cultures, and practices—biases that the FFPU and the women involved in it may challenge or reinforce. The main focus is on the policy and its implementation in practice, not its effectiveness, although the ways we talk about whether or how effective it is are also important and thus have been included in the analysis.

DATA COLLECTION AND ANALYSIS

Research for this book has involved analyzing UN documents, public discourse as presented in global media outlets, and semistructured interviews with current and former officials involved in developing or implementing policies and practice around the FFPU. I conducted the interviews in New York, at UN headquarters; in New Delhi, India, at the Indian Police Service, India's Central Reserve Police Force, and at various locations convenient for meeting scholars and former officers; and in Monrovia, Liberia, at the United Nations Mission in Liberia, via telephone, and via Skype. This information is supplemented with data gathered by a research assistant who interviewed Liberian citizens in Monrovia, Liberia, and provided information on their views of the FFPU. Interviewees were asked a number of questions from an interview schedule, though others were added or omitted as relevant in the context. Notes were taken during the interviews, which were digitally recorded. From the transcripts and recordings, the interviews were analyzed to determine how planning, deployment, and action for the FFPU took place and to locate key themes or discourses around how the FFPUs were understood by the officers involved in them, the UN, and the wider public in the deploying and host countries. The findings serve as the basis for this book.

Working across these areas follows the appeal to "study up," looking at powerful institutions and people who are elite members of their communities and organizations.[21] Yet Laura Nader, who first made this appeal in terms of ethnographic studies, makes the important point that the scope should not be limited to studying up and that better theoretical insights will come from multidimensional approaches that include studying "up, down, or sideways" depending on the terms of the problem, rather than seeing these angles as mutually exclusive.[22] Although focused on anthropological studies, Nader's insights have influenced a number of related fields, such as policy studies and sociology, and they have been useful in my own research for this book. Although trained as a political scientist, in conducting this and other research I aim to locate the appropriate concepts and tools for researching the issue at hand. Hence, throughout the book I draw on research in political science as well as on the work of scholars in other disciplines who offer rich, relevant information through ethnographic studies and other angles. Other scholars have rearticulated Nader's approach to include the concept of "studying through," which has been useful in considering public policies because it traces the ways power connects networks and actors, discourses, and institutions through space and time.[23] The research presented here begins the complex challenge of answering these questions about the FFPU and the broader political and discursive implications its presence may signal. Research on women in peacekeeping across multiple settings may make it possible to systematically identify patterns through the triangulation of experiences and observations.[24]

Moreover, research on the roles, understandings, and experiences of women in an all-female peacekeeping unit may offer valuable insights that cannot be obtained from studying male-only units or even those that involve women in small numbers. After all, Annica Kronsell found that in institutions reflecting hegemonic masculinity most women did not want to participate in research or media reports, since being singled out as women and having the differences between them and their male colleagues highlighted for all to see made them uncomfortable. Women in such contexts are often "working to not be different but to become a soldier or officer just like everyone else."[25] The subtext here may be that being "just like everyone else" in this context means being someone who can fit in as "one of the boys." We may circumvent this barrier to understanding women's participation in peacekeeping to some extent by conducting research with women working in all-female units, who may be free of this pressure, at least within their all-female spaces.

KEY THEMES

Following the feminist questions just outlined, this book focuses on telling the story of the first FFPU deployed in UN peacekeeping. In doing so, it looks at policies, attitudes, outcomes, and norms. The contribution this may make to our understandings of women, gender, and peacekeeping is important in itself, but the FFPU also draws curiosity for being unusual as an idea and a practice. Understanding it necessitates paying "attention to agency, channels of influence, strategies, and competing ideas and practices."[26] In doing so, I explicitly avoid instrumentalizing women's participation in peacekeeping by refusing to make any attempt at "measuring" the FFPU's performance against their male colleagues'. This would reflect a limited view of gender equality in peace and security, whereas I seek to think broadly about whether and how FFPUs and similar practices further gender equality, peace, and security and what difficulties they raise in society and for the direct participants.

While there may be limits to conclusions that can be drawn from focusing on the FFPUs themselves (rather than comparing them with mixed-gender units, for example) this work is required for a rich, in-depth analysis of women serving with other women.[27] Later analyses could certainly fruitfully consider FFPUs in a cross-analysis of formed police units, including mixed-gender contingents. That said, attempts to compare impacts of an FFPU to those of a mixed-gender unit would be likely to encounter significant problems, given the diverse areas of conflict in which they work, the different cultures and characteristics that constitute any given unit, and the varied interactions each unit may have with military personnel, among other things. UN Resolution 1325, passed in 2000, required member states to promote women's participation in peace negotiations and in postconflict reconstruction, but research on women in peacekeeping. has long been limited by a lack of gender-disaggregated data.[28] Scarce data, validity concerns, and structural problems all make it very difficult to "measure" the potential impacts of women's involvement.[29] To date, Resolution 1325 has led to improvements in data collection and availability, but much more remains to be done.[30]

Recognizing that women's experiences are diverse and influenced by other forms of inequality, this book also asks how such an initiative by the Indian state, staffed by Indian women, fits into broader discourses of gender equality in the international sphere, where a tendency to more highly value or regard approaches developed by Western states and women leaders that represent them has led to an unnecessarily narrow view of what steps can be taken to improve women's access to and participation in peace and security. The Indian establishment of an FFPU represents a broader, more nuanced approach to the UN's Women, Peace and Security agenda, a set of resolutions that includes Resolution 1325 and seven other resolutions passed since then to address the disproportionate effect of conflict on women.[31] Contributions such as this deserve significantly more attention than they have received to date from scholars and policy makers. This is not to suggest that the policies and practices associated with the FFPU are better for all women everywhere but rather to suggest that they may pose a good and fair option for many.

The United Nations Security Council, through the Women, Peace and Security agenda, has directly stated support for gender equality in peace and security, and in doing so has predominantly used approaches categorized as "gender mainstreaming" or "gender balance." However, progress has been limited, particularly in the peace and security realm and women's participation in peacekeeping operations specifically. Recruitment tends to target men, and gender mainstreaming often does not occur at all or is interpreted in ways that fail to improve women's positions. Indeed, some researchers have found that even those within the UN most often see the agenda as "all talk" and "not enough action" by UN bodies and member states.[32] Dominant approaches often favor gender neutrality rather than gender mainstreaming, and approaches that appear to counter "neutrality" by including involvement in "private affairs" like gender are often seen as inappropriate and thus unwelcome—even though research has found that gender-neutral approaches to legislation and policies have differing impacts on women and men and can sometimes worsen the situation for women.[33]

Those seeking to implement and expand FFPUs have faced a number of obstacles. Nonetheless, the Indian FFPU continues to inform and to give legitimacy to women's needs and concerns both as stakeholders in peace and security processes generally and as potential or actual peace-keepers. Overall, the FFPU is a potentially transformative policy while still being pragmatic. Indeed, it represents a policy innovation within the existing global gendered context. As such, it is an interesting and valuable lens for considering theories and practice around gender equality across areas such as security, political economy, and institutional cultures—all of which are discussed through the story of the FFPU told in the remainder of this book.

PLAN OF THIS BOOK

Chapter 1: The FFPU in a Global Context

Chapter 1 situates the FFPU within a complex global environment including varied and disputed approaches to gender equity and women's inclusion in peace and security initiatives. It shows how, over the past several decades in particular, significant moves have been made toward expanding and enhancing women's access to peace and security work through the United Nations. The chapter further highlights how work in this direction often remains staggered, slow, and controversial, yet clearly continues to garner support from many actors. These include women in local postconflict contexts where the UN operates, such as Liberia—the host nation for the FFPU. Liberian women have made significant contributions to peace and security, and these have been recognized both by their home country and through the UN Mission in Liberia (UNMIL). Likewise, Liberian women have taken on central leadership roles, including the presidency, and Liberia's president Ellen Johnson Sirleaf has called for and supported women's involvement in politics and peacebuilding. Understanding this global context in which the FFPU has deployed is a key first step in understanding the implications of the FFPU's work.

Chapter 2: How the FFPU Began

Chapter 2 shows how the FFPU emerged in UN peacekeeping through the contributions of several committed men and women working for the UN and the Indian government, particularly the Central Reserve Police Force and the Indian Police Service. Many of these key figures, such as Mark Kroeker, Kiran Bedi, and Seema Dhundia, acted as norm entrepreneurs, promoting the inclusion of women in policing and peacekeeping in general and promoting the creation of all-female units as a practical way to achieve greater participation by women. This approach drew on India's historical context of gendered approaches to policing, including the use of all-women's units in the Central Reserve Police Force and all-women's police stations in the Indian Police Service. Key actors such as Indira Gandhi used their political leadership and connections to enshrine such women-focused policing efforts in state policy. Such initiatives then served as inspiration for creating FFPUs that are somewhat different from the domestic police units that inspired them. At the same time, chapter 2 shows how moves toward including women and the very presence of women in policing are likely to challenge conservative gender norms in a variety of contexts and lead to contestations. It also discusses how the FFPU must be evaluated not only for its benefits to the country where it is deployed but for its benefits to FFPU officers themselves and to Indian women in the communities to which they return.

Chapter 3: Women at Work

Chapter 3 explores the key responsibility of the FFPU—providing security—and how they have carried out this role in Liberia. While facing many challenges, the FFPU have done a great deal to break down barriers to women's participation in peacekeeping in particular and peace and security in general. Through their actions (and public recognition of them), the FFPU have shown that women, including those working in women-only units, can meet and exceed expectations around providing security, both traditional law-and-order policing and policing of gender-based crimes. Their success advances the interests of women who may wish to take on careers as peacekeepers, women in postconflict zones, and women who may want the option of reporting to female security personnel. At the same time, the FFPU's presence disrupts widely accepted narratives that pressure men and boys to participate in violence in order to "prove" their manhood and that marginalize the participation of women in peace processes by limiting what roles are perceived to be "appropriate" or "natural" for women. This is a direct challenge to discourses that represent women as victims in need of protection. In acting as well-trained, capable security providers who also use nonlethal options and training that includes attention to care for victims of crime, the FFPU may unsettle existing dominant discourses around gender and peacekeeping, as they show that self-proclaimed "girls" and "mothers" can create secure environments as effectively as men, and perhaps even more effectively. Indeed, the presence of the FFPU may challenge binary views of masculinity and femininity.

Chapter 4: Political Economy, Women, and Peacekeeping

Chapter 4 considers the political economic implications of women's participation in peacekeeping. This has broader implications than simply empowering the individual women participating, because peacekeepers and peacekeeping institutions, through the peacekeeping economy, inevitably interact with and influence the societies of the countries where they are deployed. In this case the presence and practice of the FFPU might facilitate economic empowerment for women and girls in the deploying country and the host country by (1) upholding the rights of women and girls to both access and participate in security institutions, (2) supporting women's and girls' access to education, and (3) providing decent employment with comparatively high pay. But members of the FFPU, while receiving benefits from this work, perform, and are expected to perform, extra work in the form of a "second shift" of volunteer community work. Although women mostly joined the police service and the peacekeeping mission in pursuit of meaning, money, and opportunity, it has often been assumed that they should "naturally" want to and be able to spend much of their "free" time helping women and children. I do not argue that women *should* take up security sector roles or other male-dominated occupations to achieve greater economic security or recognition of full citizenship, but that participation in the security sector in general and peacekeeping in particular can open up significant opportunities for women's economic empowerment and broader pursuit of human security. Consequently states and international organizations *should* make more space for women, including reflecting on ways they may be marginalized from participation or may face extra burdens of "second shift" work even when deployed as security sector personnel.

Chapter 5: Who's Afraid of the Girls?

Chapter 5 explores how the FFPU has evoked a number of common gendered fears, including both fears about women's participation in security generally and fears about women's participation in all-female units specifically. The latter set of concerns are related to a global culture of gender mainstreaming that views women's involvement in peacekeeping as "legitimate" or "appropriate" only when it comes in the form of participating as a small minority in male-majority units. Such a limited ideology obscures the many ways that women in male-majority units have been excluded from full participation in peacekeeping; it also obscures the ways that FFPUs specifically can enhance peace and security where they are deployed. In short, efforts at including more women in peacekeeping may be limited or stalled by strict adherence to existing global culture around gender mainstreaming and a failure to critically engage with alternatives that may do more to achieve gender equity, peace and security. Moving past these limitations will require both men and women within the UN and beyond to question existing gender norms.

Chapter 6: Increasing Women's Participation in Peace and Security

Chapter 6 suggests that the FFPU could usefully be understood as an alternative interpretation of gender mainstreaming and, perhaps at least initially, be conceived of as a temporary special measure. From this perspective, further FFPUs could be developed alongside existing efforts to expand gender-integrated peacekeeping forces. Implementing such changes will not be easy or happen overnight, but addressing gender equity in peacekeeping is necessary. FFPUs appear to be a necessary step in the direction of addressing gender equity in peacekeeping, though they cannot be expected to solve all the problems women face when it comes to peace and security. Moreover, a shift in understanding is needed away from seeing women as superheroines who are naturally adapted to the task of building peace. On the contrary, the effective pursuit of peace requires work from both men and women, including peacekeepers, policy makers, humanitarian agency staff, members of community organizations, and the wider society.

The book concludes by reflecting on the stories told here of the FFPU and why they matter more broadly—including the FFPU's implications for feminist futures in UN peacekeeping—and by outlining directions for future related research.

1 The FFPU in a Global Context

It's kind of a golden age of gender work. 1325 was the push leading to it.

Department of Peacekeeping Operations official

United Nations peacekeeping has gained broad international acceptance as a mechanism for dealing with conflict and promoting peace.[1] Likewise, demand for UN peacekeeping today is higher than it has ever been and has consistently grown in recent decades.[2] Today's peacekeeping operations are multidimensional, including humanitarian, military, and police components. The transformation of peacekeeping to include this broader peacebuilding approach has further highlighted the importance of gender equality for international peace and security.[3] Today's peacekeepers work under the UN's authority to protect civilians, enable humanitarian work, and foster conflict resolution and reconciliation. Most often, they operate on the basis of three principles: "consent of the parties to the presence of the peacekeeping force, impartiality of that force, and no use of force except in instances of self-defense."[4] Within this environment, peacekeepers defend the operation's mandate, other parts of the operation, and themselves while participating in the everyday life of diplomatic, security, and local communities.[5]

The all-female formed police unit (FFPU) is one such peacekeeping unit and is overseen by the UN Department of Peacekeeping Operations (DPKO) and the UN Police Division (UNPOL). While historically UNPOL took a backseat to the military division, in recent years it has risen in status and is increasingly acknowledged as crucial for successful UN peacekeeping operations.[6] This has occurred alongside a perceived increase in numbers of what have been deemed weak states or failing states.[7] Moreover, citizens and host governments are often more accepting of police missions than military operations, which are exponentially more expensive to deploy.[8] Thus the use of formed police units (FPUs) has increased as a lower-cost way to show local populations that postconflict demilitarization is occurring while also demonstrating credibility around dealing with high-risk situations and training local police to deal with future problems.[9] At the same time, delivering police services in these cross-cultural contexts, often in unstable situations, poses significant challenges.[10]

The members of the FFPU are drawn from a paramilitary police organization (India's Central Reserve Police Force). "Policing" generally signifies law enforcement, so "paramilitary police" are understood to share characteristics of military and police institutions, which they may complement or even replace at times.[11] John Andrade defines a paramilitary force as one that "has a degree of military capability, although strictly speaking it is not a branch of an armed service."[12] However, it has been argued that all police institutions are paramilitary to some degree, though the level of militarization varies to a great extent.[13] Over recent years, police and military roles have increasingly started to converge in peacekeeping operations, both for international organizations and within particular countries.[14] The use of paramilitary police, usually understood to be a cross between normal armed forces and normal police, has been critiqued but has also been seen as necessary for limiting military participation in police activities while offering services not normally available through civil police.[15] Such groups are drawn on in UN peace operations, as FPUs are seen to "act as a key bridging unit between the military component of a peacekeeping mission and lightly-armed, often institutionally weak local police."[16]

Unlike standard police units of the UN, FPUs are recruited as a cohesive unit from an individual member state, rather than being employed by the UN as individual UNPOL officers.[17] First deployed to Kosovo and East Timor in 1999, they are intended to be more quickly deployable, better armed, and better equipped for independent operations than regular UNPOL units, allowing them to deal with diverse scenarios across the range of peace operations, especially high-risk operations.[18] They must be deployed only in full units consisting of 120 to 140 persons, or in a functional subset with a minimum of ten to twelve officers.[19] Intended to feature enhanced operational effectiveness based on the particular model of recruitment and training they use, FPUs are most often expected to fulfill three kinds of high-risk missions: managing public order, protecting UN personnel, and assisting UNPOL and local police units in especially high-risk situations.[20]

GENDER, CONFLICT, AND INSTITUTIONS

The deployment of the first FFPU in 2007 has closely followed policy developments, such as the promulgation in 2000 of the Women, Peace and Security agenda through passage of Resolution 1325, that give greater attention to the role of gender in conflict and in the establishment of peace, and the expansion of peacekeeping operations to encompass core political and economic transformations, including consideration of what have often been seen as "women's rights" or "women's issues."[21] Conflict is linked to the way genders are socially constructed; this requires analysis of the different roles of women and men in violence. One key goal is to ensure that the ideas of masculinity and femininity that are linked to violent behavior are not uncritically carried over in postconflict situations as part of daily life.[22] For example, local gender orders can play a role in feeding conflict and making peace more elusive by encouraging men and boys to participate in violence while creating disincentives for women and girls to get involved in security work. Likewise, feminist scholars, advocacy groups, and the UN have all formally recognized that creating more peaceful societies will require participation by both men and women.[23] This especially means redressing the absence of women in formal conflict resolution attempts, as substantive studies on the impact of conflict on life expectancy indicate that on average, compared to men, women are more adversely affected by civil and interstate wars.[24] In the context of the FFPU, it is thus relevant to consider whether and how women are involved in reducing violence and how this may reflect or challenge existing social constructions of gender.

Historically, war has been associated most often with men and more particularly with the characteristics expected of men—masculinities.[25] As a result, institutions tasked with military, defense, and security activities have traditionally been treated as men's property and dominated by men's bodies, a feature that has necessarily influenced the policies, politics, and agenda of security institutions.[26] Institutions tasked with security, such as the DPKO, have been widely conceptualized as sites of hegemonic masculinity, since, in addition to being dominated by men, they situate a specific form of masculinity as the norm.[27]

This book looks at FFPUs as a unique way of involving more women in the larger social structures of the UN and its subsidiary bodies. Institutional structures can be both constraining and enabling, with inner logics transcending individuals.[28] "Although structural constraints absolutely preclude the possibility of making certain choices, they also provide the basis of human thought and action, and therefore offer the very possibility of human choice."[29] Likewise, social choices can be seen as occurring "within structurally defined limits among structurally provided alternatives."[30] Agents are partly formed through institutions and most often reproduce existing structures, but the process of their doing so is always in flux, so in some times and in some ways agents may make choices that have transformative impacts on existing structures.[31] Institutions can and do change. Individuals working with and within the institutions recognize such changes and respond to them. Hence, as Kathleen Jennings has argued, it is important to understand the everyday lives and interactions of peacekeepers and the gendered form and implications of such interactions.[32] Moreover, Annica Kronsell argues that when institutions built on hegemonic masculinity take in "others," for example by including women, they may create space for the institution to develop and alter gender relations.[33] Understanding whether and how this takes place requires looking at the knowledge gained from the stories of women engaged in such institutions and at how the institutions themselves are constituted, understood, and transformed.

Since FFPUs, FPUs in general, and the paramilitary forces from which they are drawn are themselves social institutions (like families, educational institutions, or governments) and can be studied sociologically as arrangements of roles grounded in norms, beliefs, functions, and structures, multiple levels of institutions can be and are considered throughout this book to explore the intersection of broader practices and understandings of UN peacekeeping with questions of gender equity.[34] For example, the DPKO can be examined here in light of the ways it manages current social issues, such as the introduction of women into nontraditional roles. It is also useful to consider how the FFPU is situated within the broader organization of UN peacekeeping, since "professions and groups within professional institutions can be ranked in terms of power, prestige, and compensation. Also associated with these professions are popular images of their values and ways the professionals interact with each other and wider society."[35]

"In our gendered political institutions, men are the default assumption."[36] This remains the case despite an increased frequency of rhetoric around gender equality, since stereotypes that leaders must behave in masculine ways persist, as does the notion that men in general can and should embody masculine characteristics, such as rationality and lack of emotion, while women are seen as unable to do so.[37] These characteristics associated with men and masculinity are situated as neutral and "best" practice. Indeed, "With troubling frequency, *gender* is used interchangeably with *women*, conflating the two and leaving *men* as the unmarked, default category—the generic *human* against which others are compared and potentially deviate."[38] In this way supposed gender neutrality can obscure the assumptions of masculinity that make gender inequity difficult to see, or when it is seen, make it appear "natural."[39] Formal institutions may take a more conservative approach to gender equality, or one that fits more obviously with the institutional culture, which may not always line up neatly with goals of gender equality in theory or in practice. Indeed, "Institutional concepts of gender equality are shaped by the need to accommodate a broad range of positions, including those that see no need to 'fix' gender relations."[40]

Where this is the case and critical engagement is lacking about the absence of women or femininity and the related dominance of men and masculinity, international institutions like the UN may perpetuate or foster gender inequality in areas where peacekeepers are deployed. In fact, when entering postconflict countries to facilitate transitions, international organizations can import gender inequalities, especially where they fail to reflect on their own masculinist biases and perpetuate the practice of replacing men in power with other men in power.[41] Their doing so is reinforced by norms that stereotype women as homogeneous, evaluation of policy approaches according to "a logic of ranking rather than problem solving," and a tendency to label women from the global South as victims rather than agents.[42] Likewise, as Carol Harrington argues, in many ways and contexts "peacekeeping practices clearly manifest 'Western' male violence and domination."[43]

Could FFPUs challenge dominant manifestations of peacekeeping? In institutional environments where men's bodies and masculinities are seen as "naturally" dominant, including those tasked with peacekeeping, the presence of women may destabilize the institutional reliance on hegemonic masculinity.[44] More broadly, scholars studying bureaucracies have argued that a critical mass of women, typically defined as about 30 percent, can alter the operating procedures of male-dominated institutions, allowing them to strategically advance feminist strategies from the inside.[45]

It is important, however, to note that women are not homogeneous. Just as "elected female representatives will not necessarily share the same political positions," and women political representatives cannot be necessarily assumed to always "take a "pro-woman" stance" such as "in relation to the central political task of setting a national budget," women police cannot be universally assumed to act as women for women.[46] For example, in Sarah Hautzinger's study of women's police stations in Brazil, policewomen working there repeatedly told her that "a police officer does not have a sex."[47] Hautzinger did find that at times women police were expected to "sacrifice" themselves as individual women for the presumed greater good of all women. But as she noted, expecting policewomen to do gendered policing without changing the way politics and power were coded as masculine in Brazil meant that policewomen emerged as "the losers";[48] while some women were enthusiastic about their unique role, many were reluctant to assume it because they felt that the gendered division of labor and limitations on the duties they could perform would impede their future careers.[49]

Over time, Brazilian policewomen working in these specialized sections have increasingly committed to and identified with the project of women's policing, providing greater support to women complainants and improving the quality of their services.[50] But like male police, policewomen may discriminate on identity factors like race and class—gender is not stand-alone. For example, when encountering complainants they saw as coming from populations they identified as "marginal," such as poor

people or Afro-Brazilians, Brazilian policewomen often devoted significant effort to telling the complainants how the "immoral" or "improper"
activities they engaged in created the conditions for the violence they had
experienced.[51]

In the peacekeeping context factors that intersect with gender—such as
race, class, and religion—may similarly affect relations between female
peacekeepers and other women. In comparison to some other troop contributors, India might be assumed to have a strong commitment to valuing
diversity, as Indian state policy reflects a commitment to secularism, and
the troops provided are "multi-faith and ethnically diverse."[52] Nonetheless,
Marsha Henry, for example, notes that other factors certainly play a role in
the identity constructions of peacekeepers.[53] In particular, she highlights
the visible legacy of colonialization in the Indian military context, where
ethnic and caste-based differences in representation persist.[54] Henry, in
analyzing *All Girl Squad*, a BBC documentary film on the FFPU's deployment, points out that the women peacekeepers interviewed express no particular feeling of connection with the local female population and that two
of them criticize Liberians' sexual behavior and culture, viewing themselves
as more respectable. The film itself reflects this critical distance, juxtaposing
"upstanding" FFPU women with the Liberian women, who are portrayed as
"fallen" and "damaged" victims.[55]

EVOLVING APPROACHES: GENDER EQUITY,
THE WPS AGENDA, AND UN PEACEKEEPING

FFPUs have been introduced and implemented in a period when gender
has been gaining continuously greater attention in discussions around
peace and security, both domestically and internationally. At the international level, the Women, Peace and Security (WPS) agenda of the United
Nations Security Council has formally recognized the goal of women's
equal participation in peace and security initiatives as integral to achieving and sustaining peace.[56] Resolution 1325, which requires member
states to expand the roles and representation of women in the prevention
of war, in peace negotiations, and in postconflict reconstruction, is legally
binding on state signatories to the UN Charter.[57] It has led to numerous

national action plans and other policies supporting women's participation, leading some scholars to describe it as a significant move toward gender equality.[58] Although it and the subsequent seven resolutions that make up the WPS agenda (Resolutions 1820, 1888, 1889, 1960, 2106, 2122, and 2242) have sometimes been co-opted or only superficially complied with, they are important in that they reflect "a set of norms that are gradually becoming institutionalized within the UN."[59]

At the same time, one could argue that progress toward achieving gender equity in peace and security processes has been slow. Heidi Hudson's statement from over a decade ago that "progress has certainly been flawed and nonlinear" still applies.[60] This may be in part due to an overemphasis on the notion of women as victims: while there is keen interest in discussions around conflict related to sexual violence, little attention has been given to the ways women can participate in peacebuilding and conflict resolution.[61]

Moreover, although now "it is generally accepted that to include both men and women in a peacekeeping team is beneficial with respect to achieving mission objectives," a focus on instrumentalist reasons for including women dominates.[62] These reasons, which are generally based on stereotypes about women's "natural" talent for carework, limit critical engagement with barriers to women's participation in peacekeeping and the pursuit of gender equity more broadly.

Women face many such barriers to participation in masculine-identified practices of peace processes, including assumptions about their inability to participate in violent altercations, added work and family responsibilities, lack of access to education and training, and some men's reluctance to relinquish power.[63] And although Resolution 1325 has been used significantly, particularly among adult women, in their efforts at organizing, raising awareness, and advocating for gender equality,[64] some areas have seen little change. Girls' exclusion from peacebuilding programs, for example, has continued.[65] Moreover, importantly in this context, women's participation in peacekeeping overall has not altered significantly. A UN source states that as of 2004 "only some 1 per cent of the total military personnel deployed in international operations are women";[66] another gives 2010 figures as 2 percent for female military peacekeepers and 7 percent for female police peacekeepers;[67] another gives 2012 figures as 3 percent and 10 percent respectively;[68] and still another gives the same 3 percent and 10 percent figures for April 2015.[69]

In 2009, on the first anniversary of Resolution 1820, UNPOL's Global Effort was launched with the goal of reaching 20 percent women in police peacekeeping roles by 2014, a figure that would have represented a substantial increase. In particular, the initiative called on member states to "establish a policy that sets the percentage of their contribution of female police officers on a par with their national police gender ratio; [r]eview their recruitment requirements and procedures for international deployment to ensure that female candidates are not restricted from applying; and; [c]onsider providing incentives for officers who serve in peacekeeping missions."[70] This goal has not yet come close to reality. Regardless, "Merely counting women overlooks a greater complexity of why women are in minority as well as the type of impact their participation has,"[71] so critical analysis that goes beyond numbers is needed.

The failure to include more women in peacekeeping roles is significant because, as the chairperson from Ghana noted at a UN Policy Dialogue, "While the presence of women does not provide a guarantee against continued violence and return to conflict, their absence virtually ensures it."[72] A recent WPS resolution, Resolution 2122 (2013), takes the important step of seeking more than gender balance in terms of numbers: it calls for consulting as well as including women in peace talks; developing and deploying women's technical expertise in peacekeeping and mediation; and providing enhanced access, through Security Council briefings and reports, to data and research on how women are affected by conflict and how women participate in conflict resolution.[73]

THE LIBERIAN CONTEXT FOR FFPU DEPLOYMENT

The first FFPU was deployed in the UN Mission in Liberia. Liberia's fourteen years of civil war resulted in a quarter of a million civilian deaths and the displacement of 60 percent of the country's population.[74] Violence became normalized, a culture of impunity persisted, and instability and insecurity led to economic decline.[75]

Within this environment women frequently experienced violence and faced growing constraints on their equality.[76] Nonetheless, the women of Liberia engaged in a challenging political struggle to assert their rights and demand peace. When the peace process started in 2001, the Mano River Women Peace Network (MARWOPNET) and the Women in Peacebuilding Network (WIPNET) had already built up their membership significantly, and WIPNET took on the primary coordination responsibilities in the Women of Liberia Mass Action for Peace campaign, which involved women from across Liberian society in both sit-ins and formal peace negotiations.[77]

As women's groups continued to gain influence, MARWOPNET was granted observer status in the peace negotiations sponsored by the Economic Community of West African States and acted as a signatory to them.[78] When peace talks stalled in 2003, Women of Liberia Mass Action for Peace obstructed the male participants in the negotiation from leaving and demanded a swift peace agreement.[79] Their demand was met and an agreement was signed. The Comprehensive Peace Agreement included quotas for women in the Transitional Legislative Assembly, established provisions for gender balance in both elected and nonelected posts, and set the framework for including women in the country's postconflict infrastructure.[80] The UN Security Council established the UN Mission in Liberia through Resolution 1509 (2003) in order to support the peace process and implement the cease-fire agreement.[81] As of 2009, President Sirleaf reported the UN was spending $1 million per day on peacekeeping operations in Liberia.[82]

The peacekeeping mission in Liberia was the first established following passage of Resolution 1325 and has hence been seen as an important test of whether the UN is really committed to gender mainstreaming in peacekeeping practice.[83] The Liberian mandate for peacekeeping operations has received high praise from scholars advocating for gender equity—Heidi Hudson has referred to it as "the most progressive when it comes to gender mainstreaming strategies."[84] In 2005 Ellen Johnson Sirleaf became Liberia's first democratically elected woman president in an election in which over half of voters were women,[85] and many women involved in advocating for peace supported her campaign. Her original cabinet included women in several high-level ministerial appointments.[86] Since the UN mission's deployment in 2003, Liberia has held two peaceful presidential elections, the last of which took place in November 2011.[87]

This book does not make any strong claims about what such national-level female leadership means for everyday Liberian women and whether it might be evidence of gender equality. However, important work is under way in that area. A forthcoming dissertation by Michelle Dunn concludes that while Liberia has a woman president who has strongly advocated for gender equality, this has not necessarily translated to substantive change at the everyday level in Liberia. Plans and agendas exist, but their implementation is complicated by long-held traditions and divisions based on ethnicity and location (urban/rural), which are both also gendered.[88]

While WIPNET and other organizations have achieved strong gains in voter registration for women, they do not necessarily amount to an equal voice in elections or equality more generally. In the latest senatorial elections the numbers have even gone down. Women's groups are likewise often critical of the government's work on gender equality and see the absence of formal quotas as a serious issue. Even though women did make up a large proportion of votes toward Sirleaf's election, in both the 2005 and 2011 elections her win relied largely on support from male voters, including local male leaders. Campaigns continue around trying to encourage women to vote, not just for their male relatives or as male relatives demand, or in response to campaign promises of money or food ("belly-driven politics"). These challenges are compounded by the fact that the small number of women in parliament have been unable to introduce substantial political changes.[89]

In Liberia today, women still have difficulty accessing education, job opportunities, and services,[90] and one-third of Liberian girls become pregnant before reaching eighteen years old.[91] Yet through their ongoing participation and commitment to peace women have consolidated their role in the public sphere.[92] As of 2013, women made up 31 percent of senior ministers in the government, and the numbers are anticipated to continue rising.[93]

Questions remain for the future: Sirleaf has been a strong role model, yet in recent years some within the local women's movement have criticized what they see as a lack of substantive change in everyday women's lives, especially the lives of those in rural areas. In any case, Sirleaf is unable to run for reelection, and no clear leader has been identified to succeed her.

Whoever that may be, he or she will have a challenging task, since despite millions in donor funds aimed at achieving gender equality and ten years of a woman president's support of this goal, ongoing research suggests that substantial gender equality, particularly at the local level, remains to be delivered.[94]

Overall, the FFPU operates in a complex global environment that features varied and contested approaches to gender equity and women's inclusion in peace and security initiatives. Over the past several decades in particular, significant moves have been made toward expanding and enhancing women's access to peace and security work through the United Nations. Progress in this area has been slow and contested, but it continues and is supported by many actors in both local and global contexts. Women in local postconflict contexts where the UN operates, such as Liberia, have made significant contributions to peace and security, and these have been recognized both by their home countries and by UN peacekeeping missions. In Liberia, the FFPU's host country, women have taken on central leadership roles, including the presidency. The Liberian president herself, Ellen Johnson Sirleaf, has called for and supported women's involvement in politics and peacebuilding. The next chapter turns to examining how the FFPU was initiated and developed through local and global efforts.

2 How the FFPU Began

I was like an insider, so [at the UN] I told my boss, my undersecretary general, that when I go home to go to India, I'll make sure that women make it. And since then, they can't do without them. And those women have done so well in Liberia.

Former police adviser Kiran Bedi

Since all-female formed police units (FFPUs) are a policy innovation diverging from earlier approaches to gender equity in peacekeeping and other efforts at implementing the UN's Women, Peace and Security resolutions, it is worth learning whether the first FFPU was introduced as part of a broader shift in policy or as a minor exception to current practice. The answer was not immediately clear. Before, during, and after the interviews conducted at UN headquarters for this project there was some confusion among current staff as to how many FFPUs existed. Moreover, among those interviewed at the UN, none were aware of when, where, or how the idea originated and was put into action. Further investigation was warranted, since this history has not been previously reported on publicly, and apparently it has left no record in the UN's institutional memory.

Various colleagues working on issues of policing in peacekeeping suggested that former UN police adviser Mark Kroeker, who served as the UN police commissioner in Liberia in 2003 and as the UN police adviser and director of the Police Division of the Department of Peacekeeping Operations (DPKO) from 2005 to 2007, had been instrumental in devising and implementing the first FFPU policy. I thus contacted him to request an interview, which he generously granted. Kroeker took great care to insist that India be given the credit for the FFPU initiative. He also explained how he and others within the UN had requested, supported, and encouraged the FFPU's deployment.

Kroeker's story highlights how men in senior positions at the UN can play an important role in furthering initiatives to enhance women's inclusion in peacekeeping. He explained: "In New York it was more of a policy role, and I took it on myself to really be a champion for women in police operations in the UN. We had a very dismal number. It's still not very gratifying, the number of women. I was pushing the envelope whenever I could, including to police-contributing countries. I visited with the permanent members and their staffs and made a number of presentations in the Security Council."

With regard to the FFPU in particular, he explained,

> I got a visit one day from the police adviser from the permanent representative from India, and he talked about how in India they have all-women units doing crowd control, and I said, "Maybe we can get them deployed as an FPU [formed police unit]?"[1] For six, seven months I was working with them on that. It took place before I left New York, and a couple of months later I left. It was a quite exciting opportunity to see it happen. . . . I think the idea emerged during our conversation. I give credit to India. I encouraged it, recruited it.

So it appears that the original introduction of the FFPU was a joint initiative between the UN's DPKO and a member state. Comments from current UN staff did not indicate support for more widespread use of FFPUs. But Kroeker, while he was in office, wanted to expand the initiative further in the hopes that more FFPUs would increase the numbers of women participating in peacekeeping by giving women an alternative to service in male-majority units. He said: "I made a trip to Nigeria, and the president there said, 'If India can do it, we can too.' I was working on Nigeria to produce an all-woman team. . . . It's a topic people like to talk about, but until they deploy them it's all talk." Kroeker saw the FFPU as important primarily because the UN desperately needed to get an FPU out to Liberia to stabilize fragile conflict areas, but at the same time, he realized that forming a unit of around 125 women in a single stroke was a way to quickly and significantly increase women's participation in peacekeeping in accordance with the stated UN goal.

As outlined in later chapters, divergent understandings of the Indian FFPU remain at the UN, but it is clear that the FFPU was inspired by and drew upon a strong tradition of policing for women by women in India.

ORIGINS IN INDIAN APPROACHES TO GENDER EQUITY AND POLICING

Indian women's groups have actively campaigned for legal reforms to address violence against women through improved prosecution mechanisms and changes to inheritance and property laws that may make women more vulnerable to violence.[2] A 1974 report that the Indian government commissioned on Indian women helped catalyze the modern Indian women's movement, as it documented gender inequalities in the form of skewed sex ratios and gendered inequities in income, education, health care access, and political representation.[3] Taking part in preparing that report and reviewing its findings galvanized many scholars and activists to redirect the focus of their activities.[4]

Research in India has suggested that even where gender quotas have not been imposed, the presence of women in decision-making roles can have significant impacts. In particular, research suggests that increased political leadership by women can lead to positive social and economic outcomes. Nonetheless, debate remains as to which policies and practices can best achieve such changes.[5] Though these debates will continue, significant policy changes have been made in India when it comes to women's participation in policing and women's access to women police. Recently, for example, in response to "shocking levels of sexual violence against women in the capital," Delhi, in March 2015 the Indian government made the decision to reserve 33 percent of police posts for women officers in Delhi and seven other union areas that the national government wholly or partially administers. The decision applies to all future police recruitment and—along with recent legal amendments creating harsher penalties for sexual crimes—aims to make the police institutions "more gender sensitive." These moves have been well received following local and global public outrage over violence against women, especially in the wake of the widely publicized 2012 incident in which a medical student was gang-raped on a Delhi bus and later died.[6]

The first FFPU in UN peacekeeping emerged from an Indian context that has historically included, and continues to include, gendered approaches to policing. Specifically, India offers the option for women to participate in and report to all-women police stations (AWPSs) or units. Despite the global publicity around the FFPU, the Indian domestic factors that made it possible have not been well recognized abroad.

Women have been involved in policing in India for many years and in many ways. Although they were working in policing in India as early as 1938, women mainly served as social workers as opposed to police officers, and even then they mainly dealt only with children and other women.[7] However, in recent decades more women have joined both the Central Reserve Police Force (CRPF), from which the FFPU is drawn, and the Indian Police Service (IPS). The increase in women's involvement, however, has been notably quicker in some Indian states than others,[8] highlighting the importance of local conditions in influencing policy and practice outcomes. Moreover, while both the CRPF and the IPS feature women's units, they have done so in different ways and for different reasons.

Women in the Central Reserve Police Force

According to a CRPF official interviewed, in 1986 the first CRPF all-female unit, the Eighty-Eighth Battalion, or Mahila ("Ladies") Battalion, was introduced with three units. He added, "There are now six thousand women in CRPF security and another two thousand in the political staff of CRPF, so there are eight to nine thousand women in the CRPF overall now." When asked why this division had been created in the CRPF, he explained that "women were needed for checking women, because to check terrorist hideouts the male police faced problems for frisking and checking women. The women said they [male police] were harassing them or had an indifferent attitude to them, so a need was felt and the women's battalion created for checking women." Thus women-specific policing units were created in the CRPF on the basis of both instrumentalist and rights-based arguments.

Another CRPF official, a former FFPU commander, further said of the first CRPF all-female unit, "We in fact are credited with having the first all-women paramilitary battalion in Asia." She recounted that the Mahila Battalion had been the idea of the late prime minister (1984–89) Rajiv

Gandhi in 1985. Specifically, she explained, "He struck upon this idea because he realized that a lot of women are taking part in the law-and-order problems around the country. They'd become part of mobs. They'd become part of processions. They'd become . . . part of all kinds of situations. So he wanted a[n] . . . all-women force who could tackle them."

This, she said, was "because the constitution . . . the law says that if you have to . . . arrest a woman you ought to have a . . . policewoman or otherwise you are not supposed to touch her." In fact, "You cannot keep a woman in custody in a police station beyond sunset. . . . So therefore, in order to . . . have somebody who could tackle women mobsters [and so on], he decided that we will have a paramilitary force and raise an all-women battalion. And its responsibility was assigned to the Central Reserve Police Force. And that is how this all-women battalion was raised in 1986."

While unfortunately there is only such limited information available on how women's roles have evolved in the CRPF, more reporting is available for the IPS initiative of creating all-women police stations (AWPSs).

Women in the Indian Police Service

AWPSs first emerged in the Indian state of Kerala in the 1970s when Indira Gandhi introduced them.[9] According to Thomas Isaac and Michael Tharakan, since the mid-1970s some have deemed Kerala worthy of being an international model, as despite low rates of economic development the state has enacted progressive social policies and achieved comparatively high rates of women's emancipation, education, and health. In particular, they spoke of working *with* the local cultural context and viewing it as part of the capacity for change that was possible in the state.[10] Kerala has not seen any organized opposition to educating girls, and the strong matrilineal traditions in the region may contribute to more progressive attitudes around women's roles.[11] In fact, women in Kerala enjoy health and literacy rates equal to males' and have not faced some of the gender discrimination that is widespread across the rest of India. Kerala is also the only state in which women are favored by the sex ratio, which everywhere else in India is skewed to a male majority.[12] The "Kerala model" has thus been widely heralded. Enthusiasm has been tempered by later economic stagnation that arguably slowed down welfare gains. Nonetheless, the impacts of Kerala

AWPSs have spread more widely throughout India and now, with the introduction of FFPUs, into international peacekeeping.[13]

In the decades that followed the creation of AWPSs, there were still only very few women in the IPS. Mainly they were responsible for searching female offenders and occasionally interviewing female victims.[14] In other words, their presence was predominantly justified in instrumentalist terms: they were there when women were seen as *necessary* to do an existing job *better*—the job of providing security in the historical, conservative sense of the term, which is concerned with traditional security as opposed to notions of human security or other frameworks that might value women's rights to be safe and free as women. In Kerala the first female police officers were reportedly seen as being needed to deal with women prisoners and to disperse and arrest women demonstrators.[15]

In 1992 the government established all-women police units (AWPUs) in the state of Tamil Nadu, in 1992.[16] They were considered a success and were extended to other Indian states as AWPSs; there are now 524 in India.[17] Originally the women police assigned to AWPSs were trained separately from men, their training emphasized counseling skills more than traditional police roles, and their jobs were solely with women and children.[18] Likewise, the AWPSs were located apart from standard police stations, so that women might feel more comfortable to come to them when crimes had been committed against them.[19]

In 1995 the National Policy for Empowerment of Women was drafted, actualizing the constitutional guarantee against sexual discrimination; it was followed by equal opportunity legislation requiring 33 percent of recruits for government jobs to be women.[20] This necessarily included the police sector and thus set a major precedent for the expansion of women's roles in policing in India. In the context of protecting women's rights to security, AWPSs have developed a number of areas of specialization, including dealing with Eve-teasing (harassment of girls), suicides, bride burnings, dowry deaths, killings due to suspicions of witchcraft, and human trafficking.[21]

Research has indicated that AWPSs provide officers well trained in providing empathetic advice and assistance.[22] Likewise, women who have been victims of crime have indicated greater willingness to report crimes because of the existence of AWPS and their feeling more comfortable reporting in such conditions.[23] Indeed, data suggest that women prefer to bring their complaints to women police, who they expect will be better able to understand and attend to the issues.[24] Extensive case records and victim interviews have also indicated that many cases were in fact "successfully resolved and violence was frequently reduced."[25]

This suggests that the AWPS could be seen as a success from an instrumentalist standpoint for addressing and prosecuting crimes and from a rights standpoint for upholding women's rights of equal access to security as well as roles in security, a significant aspect of important public sector work. Indeed, many have called the initiative a success, given the availability of specialized policing and the achievement of high response rates in areas that previously exhibited low levels of awareness about gender-based violence.[26] Similar approaches in other contexts have also been documented as successes. For example, Brazil's women's police stations have been called "a vast improvement in police responsiveness to violence against women."[27]

However, AWPS programs have had their limitations and setbacks. These are not limited to the Indian context, though it is worth considering which barriers have emerged in the Indian context as well as how they have been or remain to be addressed. Indian AWPSs have not necessarily proven to have beneficial effects on women's standing overall in the IPS or in all individual careers. Decades after the introduction of the AWPS, women still make up a tiny percentage of the overall police force and continue to face discrimination there.[28] Moreover, given the limited issues AWPSs can address, and women's widespread reluctance to report any crimes (including those not covered by the AWPS) to the standard, male-dominated stations, more remains to be done. Furthermore, women working in AWPSs have to deal with secondary traumatic stress associated with considerable work around traumatic and violent crimes against women and children, negative media portrayals of AWPS personnel, excessive impacts of the job on their family lives, and lack of respect from male police for performing different roles.[29] This has had significant impacts on whether and how the women involved can do their jobs.

For example, in Tamil Nadu, male police who assumed that women police's duties in AWPSs were less onerous than their own threatened a strike if women were not assigned the same conditions and responsibilities as men. Thus in 1997 female police recruits began training alongside male recruits and were placed in regular police battalions.[30] Likewise, many women police have experienced working in traditional police stations before taking up work in AWPSs. This has resulted in some mixed views. By 2000, women officers in AWPSs suggested they would prefer to undertake a variety of responsibilities rather than solely the limited roles assigned for AWPSs.[31] Nevertheless, though they hoped for broader roles and responsibilities, "Most of the women noted preference for the AWPS, describing better support from their fellow women police."[32] In other words, many "said they would like to perform a range of police activities, but they would like to do this in units staffed only by women."[33]

This suggests that proponents of a rights-based approach, should consider that that at least some women may be more willing to join, or remain in, the security sector when given the option of working at least some time in women-only units. And even those taking an instrumentalist approach must acknowledge that if at least some women are needed to provide security effectively, their desire for women-only units should be met. AWPS officers "continue to play important roles for women and children,"[34] as do many female police officers and other security sector professionals around the world. Looking deeply at how and why women get involved in policing and the barriers to their involvement or continuation in policing is important. Meanwhile, the information available on the Indian experience supports J. Ann Tickner's point that "when women fight for their rights, they generally get less support than when they are perceived as victims. This is because gender justice demands profound structural changes in almost all societies, changes that would threaten existing elites along with existing political, social, and economic structures... There is less risk in portraying women as victims than in supporting their empowerment. The image of helpless victims ... is politically less risky than supporting articulate forceful advocates of women's rights."[35] Such attitudes appear at the global level as well.

MAKING THE LEAP FROM DOMESTIC TO INTERNATIONAL IN THE POLICY REALM

How did the concept of all-women's units go global? Looking at the FFPU's history provides a chance to consider how unique domestic conditions in India were translated into an international policy innovation in

UN peacekeeping. Indeed, this case exemplifies how "the frontier between domestic and foreign policy is ever porous and frequently transgressed,"[36] and it is worth considering why this is so.

A range of international conventions and resolutions suggest that some level of international agreement exists between states around women's rights to equality, nondiscrimination, participation, and inclusion as broadly defined. However, women's ability to access these rights is contested both locally and globally, within and between states. In recent decades, this contestation has necessarily occurred alongside the spread of neoliberal economic systems, which have arguably eroded the power and centrality of the state, while spreading a dominant discourse of market-based solutions and individual approaches that ignore structural impediments. Within this environment, states can and do operate in multifaceted ways domestically and in the international sphere—they may act to limit women's access to their rights at home or abroad, but at the same time they can function as promoters of women's rights in the global community.

While peacekeeping is generally seen as an international activity, in practice it works as a federation of individual state troop contributions that remain mostly under state direction. Although global implementation of the UN's Women, Peace and Security agenda has been nonlinear and slow, states can at times provide alternative pathways that may sidestep some of the "blue tape" to achieving gender equity through the United Nations. India's introduction of the FFPU appears here as a clear example, yet, as will be shown later in this book, it too has faced challenges at the UN.

From the 1950s up to the present, India has been a consistent, major actor in UN peacekeeping worldwide.[37] It is one of the top three troop-contributing countries in UN peacekeeping. In recent years, police forces such as the FFPU have emerged as a major part of India's UN peacekeeping contributions. Police deployments follow the same procedures as the military deployments before them, except that the Home Ministry is the central ministry involved, rather than the Ministry of Defense.[38] Participation in peacekeeping is among India's most visible contributions to the UN, and Indian troops have served in forty out of sixty-five UN peace operations to date.[39] By April 2013, Indian peacekeepers made up just short of 10 percent of all uniformed peacekeepers working in blue-helmet operations.[40] This notable level of participation reflects a constitutional "commitment to international peace and security" and a long-standing commitment since World War II to support decolonization efforts.[41]

Thus Richard Gowan and Sushant Singh argue that according to many, "India is now the 'backbone' of UN peacekeeping."[42] At the same time, they highlight that this is not necessarily "an easy status to enjoy. Because India is such an important part of the UN peacekeeping system, its decisions over the deployment of its forces are subject to particular scrutiny."[43] Some scrutiny appears to be merited, most particularly the actions of some actors in all-male units in the Democratic Republic of Congo, where widespread, persistent reports of corruption and misbehavior, including sexual misconduct, led to investigations by an Indian army court.[44] Amid these accusations of underperformance, India rotated new contingents into the Congo but also countered criticism from Western countries by highlighting Western countries' refusal to send their own troops there and saying that India had not been adequately consulted on how its troops would be used.[45]

Given its peacekeeping experience, strengths, and reputation, India is seen by some as having credible authority to lead new directions in peacekeeping thinking, yet it has had difficulty gaining the recognition needed for such leadership.[46] One challenge in leading around initiatives aimed at improving gender equity (such as the FFPU) is that—like the other top troop-contributing countries Bangladesh and Pakistan—India has not been perceived as providing substantial attention to WPS issues, partially because of its lack of a national action plan on Resolution 1325.[47] Much work remains to be done on a global scale to ensure effective implementation of Resolution 1325, and India is of course one piece of that puzzle. However, given that currently only fifty-seven countries have national action plans, India certainly does not stand out significantly in this regard.[48]

Moreover, given that their introduction of the FFPU in Liberia has seen that country reach the highest proportion of women police in a mission, a case can be made that India has taken national action on gender equity in peacekeeping, regardless of the fact that it did not emerge as a result of a national action plan. Significantly, at the domestic level the Indian state has taken clear action to reallocate "human and/or monetary resources in order to build specialized institutions or programs that address violence against women,"[49] and it has gone even further to translate this into international peacekeeping contributions. This is an undeniably important move showing clear leadership on the issue. But how and why did India decide to take this lead? As noted previously, it was partly because of encouragement from the current (at the time) police adviser at the UN. At the same time, significant work was being done on the Indian side by another key elite actor, or norm entrepreneur, former UN police adviser Kiran Bedi.

Several officials and scholars directed me to speak to Kiran Bedi about her role in the implementation of the first FFPU, and after reading her book and watching a documentary on her life I was able to interview her. As the first ever woman officer in the IPS, and still the IPS's highest-ever ranked woman, Bedi possesses a wealth of valuable knowledge concerning women and policing in India. Moreover, having served as police adviser at the UN's DPKO in New York, Bedi was in a uniquely advantageous position to translate Indian ideas into international contributions.

Like Kroeker, Bedi was able to support this initiative as police adviser at the UN, but she could also leverage her personal contacts at the UN and within India to help make the necessary links for actually getting the FFPU idea implemented. This is a particularly interesting example of facilitating significant change. Jacqui True and Michael Mintrom have argued that "actors embedded in transnational networks are having a significant impact on domestic politics and policy."[50] In doing so, they have looked predominantly at the UN and women's international nongovernmental organizations, and they credit the transnational feminist movement with making significant gains in diffusing the norm of gender mainstreaming bureaucracies within states. While noting that this work they have identified is very important, my research on the FFPU shows that significant change can also move from the state bureaucratic level to the international level and that this can be and has been facilitated by highly connected and influential individuals such as Kiran Bedi. As noted previously, she explained, "I was like an insider, so [at the UN] I told my boss, my under-secretary general, that when I go home to go to India, I'll make sure that women make it. And since then, they can't do without them. And those women have done so well in Liberia."

From her work at the UN in New York, Bedi explained that she could see a bigger picture of peacekeeping, including the unique ways India could contribute on the basis of its existing skills and resources and where it could seek to develop further: "It really helped me, because I could now compare my own system with the world around and see what were my strengths and my weaknesses, how do we improve the system. It . . . absolutely grooms you for human rights and human responsibilities. And it opens up the world. It also tells you to be proud of what you see. I would now go back and see what were the strengths of Indian policing which we must build on and what are the areas we need to borrow and learn from." Moreover, on pursuing FFPU policy in the Indian context, Bedi explained,

> I got it initiated because I knew India had this . . . formed unit and . . . it's so effective. It's well trained, well motivated, and men alone were going [to serve as peacekeepers deployed by India]. Women were not given the option. So when I went and called upon the home minister, saying, "Well, India has this and we send men. Why can't we just replace one company or one platoon or one formation by women? We have it." And he liked the idea and he said, "Why not?" So that's when the policy changed. You see, it was male-controlled . . . policy and only male[s] promoting policy. Here came a woman who said, "Let men go, but don't hold back women. You've got them and India has it."

At the time Bedi knew she would probably face barriers, including the objection that India did not have enough women police to spare for an international mission, but she pressed forward: "The fact is that I knew India could spare. But you see, again, if you had gone bureaucratically, men could have said, "We can't spare." But . . . I was an insider. I knew India could spare. And I also knew that . . . women would love to come. See? They would love to come. And secondly, I also knew that the battalion, from which women would be brought in, would like it. So there would not be a local resistance. All it needed was a policy decision."

Leading the campaign to create India's first FFPU meant using her own skills, connections, and resources to advocate for domestic support, which required surmounting existing obstacles to turning the idea into a reality. As she recalls, "I broke those barriers. Instead of going through bureaucracy, I called on the home minister and told him, 'During your time you can get this.' You know, I made him buy an idea that would belong to him, so I said, 'Sir, this is what's happening,' and the fact that I was police adviser to the secretary general was a matter of pride for my country too, so they were listening to me. And I said, 'Why shouldn't I use this position to change things for the better?'"

Thus, she said, when planning a launch for a new training program, she called the home minister to invite him. And on that call she said, "Sir, this is an opportunity, would you like to announce this as a policy change?"

> So . . . I got the male bureaucrats out, or else there would be nothing but a file [with] a decision and pros and cons, [such as] "A woman [deployed in peacekeeping] could be threatened, a woman be raped, a woman could be . . . ," so all nonsense. So . . . I straight away went up to him and said, "Sir, if you send a formed unit, all these bureaucratic apprehensions would be out, India would make a splash . . . Indian women cops would stand out . . . They've delivered. They're very good, and it will be very good for the country and the world over. So you've got your strength, why hold it back? And if you also send men, just hold that many men back . . . you send Indian military. Let the military be army [men] and let the cops be women." So I said, "Let's balance it and our women will also get exposure, which they don't get otherwise." So you see . . . I gave him all those points, which was everything politically correct . . . It had to be politically correct, so I . . . told him, "Could you please, sir, announce this when you launch this . . . international training seminar on peacekeeping in Delhi?" So that was a great opportunity.

Bedi's comments here show an awareness of the political climate around peacekeeping, which has also been documented in scholarly analyses that portray India's rising prominence in peacekeeping as its chance to develop a "brand" as a responsible state through positive publicity for some deployments, including the FFPU.[51] Similar suggestions have been made in analyses of Brazil's women's police stations, as the concept was seen as appealing both to politicians' ambitions and to their constituencies, offering a chance to instill national pride in a country that had experienced negative effects of a "mixed international image."[52] In this sense, the FFPU may be like other units that "provide useful advertisements for India's growing strength."[53] In fact, Dipankar Banerjee suggests that a key factor in India's participation in UN operations is its "sense of being a great power in the making."[54] Likewise Gowan and Singh suggest that by engaging in peacekeeping India has seized the opportunity to engage in political leadership at the UN and portray itself as leading the bloc of troop contributors.[55] Furthermore, the state has recognized the possibility that the significant positive effects on India's international image have "helped to further its foreign policy objectives."[56] This is yet another instrumentalist argument for supporting women's participation in peacekeeping.

By leveraging her political knowledge and contacts, Bedi was thus able to get onboard another key actor who could help her attain the goal of creating and deploying an FFPU. As she put it,

> Once he [the home minister] announced it . . . saying, "We propose to do this," the bureaucrats had to fall in line. So what he did was, he went a step further and he called all the bureaucrats for a meeting and he asked me to explain it to them in his presence. And once I explained it to them in his presence, the bureaucrats would nod. And the next time, the formed unit was done. So it was diplomatically cleared, it was politically cleared, bureaucratically cleared. I cut out years of decision making by those two, three meetings and that announcement. So it worked. I had to push it because otherwise women would never have come.

Of course, from there, several practical steps were needed to put the FFPU into practice. These included recruiting, training, and deploying the unit, as well as preparing the mission for their arrival.

MOVING FROM THEORY TO PRACTICE

Although the Indian FFPU deployed in Liberia emerged from the historical and social context of Indian policing, and although the FFPU is recruited from India's CRPF, it differs from other CRPF all-female teams because it has no formal gender-specific duties. It also differs from the IPS's AWPSs in that its aim is not solely to serve women, though its extracurricular community activities may arguably be more accessible to women and children. Indeed, women police officers may be accessible to broader populations in many cases. Many young people I met in India, including men, when hearing about my project told me their views that women police were more honest, less likely to take bribes, and better at doing their jobs than male recruits. Of course, it is clear that both women and men are needed as community role models in dealing with conflict and that more research is needed on how both are understood by the populations they are tasked with serving and protecting. But how did the FFPU go from an idea to a policy directive, to a reality?

According to CRPF officials, the directive to initiate the FFPU was given to the CRPF and filtered down the chain of command. Part of this meant recruiting the first FFPU commander, Seema Dundhia, who was asked and who accepted the challenging task of putting the unit together and preparing them for being deployed. Overall, the process took seven months. After the decision was made to create the FFPU, two weeks of significant work were required to recruit women for the contingent from the existing ranks of the CRPF. This involved putting together a selection process, which included conducting physical fitness testing and working with psychiatrists and counselors to administer extensive tests to ensure that those selected would be physically, psychologically, and emotionally capable of doing the job well and would prove resilient in spending such a considerable time away from their families and homes. Those selected then underwent extensive training over six months, which included learning about the logistics and equipment for their deployment, as well as receiving information about the history and current situation in Liberia since the conflict. Upon completing their training, the FFPU members also all needed to pass the UN Special Police Assessment Team test before being cleared to deploy to Liberia.

Putting together appropriate training required a great deal of resourcefulness on the part of the FFPU commanders, as they had not been given clear information on what the UN wanted from their unit. Some of this involved doing research for themselves online to learn more about the Liberian conflict and context and devising survival strategies based on what they could learn there. The commander also went to Liberia prior to deployment to meet with the special representative to the secretary general, operational commanders, and the FPU coordinator. By doing her research on that trip she was able to get a fair idea of her prospective troop's logistical needs to convey to others as appropriate. She then wrote a report on what she had learned there to provide to her CRPF director and the ministry. A meeting on the report followed at UN headquarters to verify that everything was on track to proceed. This included the director general meeting with UN officials to finalize the memorandum of understanding for the unit to move toward final deployment.

Once this was agreed on, CRPF officers could proceed with selecting troops and purchasing, organizing, and shipping equipment to Liberia. In all they sent seventeen containers filled with necessary items such as weapons and ammunition, including nonlethal weapons. The commander also requested catering and laundry services from the UN side, explaining that her troops would be too busy managing their jobs. "What are we going to do," she asked, "if they really have to do all sort of laundry and cleaning and all?" This line of questioning showed the commander's awareness that this would be a second shift for the women that would take excessive time away from their duties, which included providing security 6.5 days per week. However, the UN did not provide these services. Consequently, in a turn that significantly challenged gender stereotypes of how men and women operate in peace operations contexts, the Indian contingent decided to recruit a small number of men to take with them to perform jobs like cooking and cleaning.[57]

The introduction of the FFPU succeeded not only because Indian officials worked to make it happen but also because many people offered support through their roles in the UN. For example, one former DPKO official explained, "It takes a lot more than an idea. A lot of people were involved in consensus building. . . . Deputy SRSG Luiz [Carlos] de Costa . . . in Liberia was eagerly pushing to have them deployed. . . . They were eager to have them."

Likewise, Lt. Sal Rodriguez, the FPU coordinator in Liberia at the time of the first FFPU's deployment, explained that a lot of collaboration went into getting the contingent into place.

> We [I and the deputy police commander, a Norwegian woman] went to the FPU leadership conference and met . . . the first female FPU commander. She said she was trying to get an FFPU going but was meeting with a lot of resistance. I went and met with her and the commander. The commander then makes the stuff move faster. I started turning the wheels on the logistical side at UNMIL [the UN Mission in Liberia]. I helped build three camps. . . . Dhundia and General Dey were in charge of tactical units in India, and a lot of credit goes to them. There was a real women's movement in police work there, and he [General Dey] wanted India to be represented by women.

Rodriguez also took the FFPU commander's requests on a flash drive with lesson plans, Power Points, and related resources to train the relevant UN staff already in Liberia so they would be prepared for the FFPU's arrival. He received help with logistics, training, and assessment from another man working in police peacekeeping, from the gender adviser of the mission's police force, and from an ambassador, who was instrumental in getting support from the US State Department. These men and women working in a variety of roles in relation to the UN helped create the material conditions that made the deployment possible. Once all of this planning and negotiation was complete, the FFPU traveled to Liberia to begin their mission.

EVERYDAY LIVES IN EXTRAORDINARY CIRCUMSTANCES

Upon arrival in Liberia, the contingent and the base were established, and the accommodations were reviewed, modified, and settled into over a period of four to five months, which included several visits from the special representative to the secretary general. During the initial stages the FFPU members continued training through daily presentations about the mission, codes of conduct, and requirements of their work. Beyond the official UN examinations they had completed, the women were again tested on what they had learned, this time in a very real context. As the commander explained,

> In fact, the very first day when we were deployed there in Liberia, the day we landed . . . there was a huge mob of ex-combatants, so that was our testing time because even [the UNMIL FPU coordinator] told us, "Now ladies, this is your testing time. It's going to be the first exposure to the Liberian people as well to the UN, you know, other elites." So, I think, don't worry. We will prove our worth. Don't worry. But it really gets difficult sometimes because people are so apprehensive, so critical in their approach, you know, they really want to see whether these females are really going to perform or are they going to succeed or to fail or what, what, how are they going to react to, in the situation.

At first, she said, it was a challenge to respond to the many apprehensions some people in the mission appeared to have about their presence. But the women of the FFPU persevered and gained the respect of many skeptics: "In the beginning there were, it was not a sort of challenge, but apprehensions, of course. . . . They were very apprehensive. They say, 'Oh, the females have arrived. What are they going to do?' . . . But later on, when we told them very categorically that we mean business and . . . we can also handle such situations . . . , that feeling . . . subsided and it wasn't there.

[The apprehension was] just in the beginning maybe fifteen, twenty days, and then later on it [dissipated]."

The FFPU also faced other unique challenges, including local diseases they had not been adequately informed about so that they could make the needed preparations to protect themselves—even though the leadership had done everything they could to inform themselves and their unit and take precautions. They knew that medical facilities in the mission area would be very sparse, and they had been told the area was rife with Lassa fever and a particularly resistant strain of malaria. The doctors in the team had read extensively on what kinds of diseases might be prevalent in the mission area and how to deal with them should they arise. Still, they encountered other diseases they had never seen before, including a skin disease called miasis, which is spread by the tsetse fly as it lays its eggs on the skin. The eggs travel through the skin and become larvae, disturbing the patient as they start moving beneath the skin. This caused a scare among the FFPU troops, most of whom had never been on an international mission or even left India. As a commander recounted,

> That was the first time we had seen such a thing, and one of my girls got infested with that. [One] morning I got this information that one of my girls was having this problem, and most of my troops . . . they said they don't want to stay in Liberia because . . . they could see . . . that thing happening to one of their colleagues. So . . . it was a very tough time for me because it took almost two days for me to convince them that see, it is curable, perfectly all right after they have taken care of it. You don't have to worry. Because most of my girls, you know, they started telling [me], "We want to go back. We don't want to stay here." But . . . somehow it was managed, and later on they also got used to it, that it was just a simple thing. . . . It was totally curable, but initially, you know, it just gave a shock to my troops. We were all shocked. They said they never wanted to be there, they just want to come back home, but these are situations that are sometimes with the team.

Despite all of the challenges, the first FFPU were able to return home to India with all of the contingent safe and sound, which the commander said for her "was the biggest achievement" and something for which she was very grateful. "If somebody asked me," she said, "'What was the achievement?' I [would] say, 'I took 125 personnel to Liberia and I got them back safe and sound. That was the biggest achievement.'" Indeed, it is no surprise that she saw this as significant, for "India has the unhappy distinction of losing more personnel on UN missions than any other nation";[58] as of January 31, 2012, it had racked up "143 fatalities on UN missions."[59] The loss of Indian peacekeeping personnel in Somalia had led to questions about India's ongoing commitment to providing peacekeepers,[60] and attacks resulting in peacekeeper deaths in the Democratic Republic of Congo had led to questions about whether the Indian peacekeepers had been adequately trained and prepared for the tasks they faced.[61] Hence, the commander's pride in successfully training her unit to ensure their safety seems well founded.

The first FFPU was an achievement in broader terms as well. After initially deploying for six months, the unit had their mission extended to one year, and the decision was made to continue the practice by bringing in a second FFPU to replace them when they returned home. This rotation process has been ongoing since the first FFPU in 2007, with India introducing new troops in the first quarter of each year to ensure an ongoing Indian FFPU presence in UNMIL.

Just as the everyday lives of the first FFPU members had significant impacts on whether and how they would take part in peacekeeping and how those around them would interpret this, this has also been the case for the FFPUs that have rotated in after them. Both because women's private roles in the family have been invoked to create heightened, often inaccurate expectations of women in peacekeeping, and because private lives influence whether and how all peacekeepers will undertake their duties and affect local communities, aspects of everyday life matter in this analysis. As Kathleen Jennings has argued, it is important to understand the everyday lives and interactions between peacekeepers and local communities, as well as the gendered form and implications of such interactions.[62]

Through their everyday lives and interactions the FFPU has effected some significant changes. Their very presence makes gender visible whereas previously peacekeeping was assumed to be the "natural" domain of men and masculinity. Their presence as peacekeepers and their high visibility as an all-women's unit challenge gender dichotomies and break down stereotypes. This is important because when women take part in conflict they can reinforce militarization, and when they act solely as peacemakers they can reinforce militarized masculinity and the marginal role women are typically seen as occupying in the security sector.[63] This narrow approach to women's roles in wars can reify traditional ideas about femininity and serve as a justification for wars.[64] Yet the highly visible presence of women in a paramilitary police unit tasked with peacekeeping confounds such stereotypes and assumptions. Most notably, the success of the FFPU shows that effective leadership requires not only participation by men and women but also both masculine and feminine traits within individual leaders.

The qualities of a woman and a competent security worker are often viewed as inherently antithetical,[65] but FFPU members break down stereotypes by standing out as women doing security in the context of their everyday lives. Before I visited the FFPU at their compound in Congotown, Monrovia, a UNMIL staff member in the police division shared with me that the compound had once been the home of former Liberian president and convicted war criminal Charles Taylor. The staff member said the FFPU commander's office was Taylor's former workspace and suggested that "the carpet in that room has probably been changed a few times," highlighting the many killings that reportedly occurred there and the graphic history the FFPU would have to contend with in their daily lives as peacekeepers.

When I arrived at the compound, I was surprised to notice that one of the women who escorted me (an officer in the FFPU) was wearing electric blue nail polish that matched her uniform. Small details like this made it stand out that I had arrived at a women's unit. The women of the FFPU invited me in for lunch after my meetings and gave me a scarf from India as a gift. This was the first time in my research with the security sector that I had ever received a fashion accessory, and the significance was not lost on me. Having previously attended male-dominated conferences and workshops filled with men in uniform, where I was highly aware of the need to avoid appearing "too feminine," I was reminded of how the few women in attendance at such conferences would often joke in the breaks that the best part of being there was that at these conferences, unlike any other time in our lives, we could walk right into the ladies' room, while unfortunately the men had to queue for the toilets. Doing research in an all-female unit was noticeably different. As a woman in research around peace and security who had experienced my fair share of male-dominated spaces, I felt much more at ease about fitting in or being accepted in the space, knowing that I would not be taken less seriously simply for being a woman. While this is merely my own experience, at least some other women may at times feel similarly. For some, accessing a unit or station staffed completely by women may indicate that women are taken seriously here and that it is an okay space to be a woman. This is important because it has certainly not been the case for many spaces where women are expected to report crimes or work to prosecute them.

While those critical of women's involvement in traditionally male occupations that are physically demanding have historically questioned the biological capacity of women to perform in these arenas, the FFPU has shown that any claims that women cannot meet the physical standards to perform as peacekeepers are unfounded. At or near their compound in Congotown, FFPU officers do physical training every day first thing in the morning and maintain a visibly high level of fitness. One officer runs marathons in her spare time, which is limited given that they, like other local UN officials, work 6.5 days per week. The commander at the time of my visit described herself as a "jack of all trades" in the sports arena. Growing up, she said, she had always been outside, being active, and coming in sunburned. She had played basketball in high school and said when it came to sports she liked to do them all and could play well on the field but did not specialize in one so would not captain any, despite her leadership credentials. Her stories and others highlight that many women enjoy and can excel in the physical challenges police officers are required to meet.

The women leading the FFPU make clear that their leadership is dependent on being skilled, competent professionals. For many, this is something they balance with other family commitments and responsibilities. For example, the outgoing commander's husband was also an officer in the CRPF, and she had two daughters aged ten and twelve. As she was preparing to hand over her leadership of the FFPU to the incoming commander, she told me of her hope that upon her return she would be posted to the same area her husband was in so they could see each other more often. Such stories illustrate that the first FFPU that deployed in 2007 and all those that have followed in their footsteps are doing challenging and important work around integrating their personal lives and experiences into their roles as peacekeepers. Through resourcefulness, commitment, and resilience, the officers of the FFPU have clearly shown themselves up to the challenge of meeting and exceeding expectations. Furthermore, the deployment and widely perceived success of the FFPU in Liberia may contribute to the continuation and expansion of all-women's units and stations within India, as "coordination with international organizations can help to provide pressure to increase responsiveness, but also provide funding that is often necessary to create or sustain specialized institutions."[66]

As this chapter has shown, the FFPU emerged in UN peacekeeping through the work of several committed individuals, both men and women, working for the UN and the Indian government, particularly the CRPF and the IPS. Many of these key actors, such as Mark Kroeker, Kiran Bedi, and Seema Dundhia, acted as norm entrepreneurs, promoting the inclusion of women in policing and peacekeeping in general and promoting the creation of all-female units as a practical way to achieve greater participation by women. This approach drew on India's historical context of gendered approaches to policing, including the use of all-women's units in the CRPF and AWPSs in the IPS. Key actors such as Indira Gandhi, who used her political leadership and connections to enshrine these women-focused policing efforts in India's state policy, also had important roles to play in starting initiatives. Once in place in the Indian domestic context, gendered policing initiatives served as inspiration for creating novel approaches to pursuing gender equity in UN peacekeeping through the use of women's units that are in some ways similar to but in others different from the Indian units that inspired them.

The stories of the first FFPU and those that have followed show that the FFPU has faced challenges both as people (the troops) and as a policy. The women involved have worked hard to integrate their experiences and lives into their roles as peacekeepers and have managed to meet and indeed exceed expectations. Moreover, the Indian case shows how it is important to consider the effects of all-women's units on both women in the community and women police themselves. Beulah Shekhar and Vivian Lord have argued that "the status of AWPS[s] in India should be considered from the benefits that they provide women citizens of India, but also the progress, or inhibition of progress for the women police assigned to the AWPS."[67] This same claim can be usefully and logically extended to all-female units in UN peacekeeping. After all, the Indian case shows that both instrumentalist and rights-based logics and evaluations may be and have been used at different times in to justify (or criticize) women's policing initiatives. In

Tamil Nadu, for example, once gender quotas in policing were established, male police, who presumably felt the perceived loss of their privilege and status, resorted to a strike, demanding that women police take on the same duties as men and serve alongside them. This highlights one of the ways the very presence of women in policing is likely to challenge conservative gender norms in a variety of contexts. Despite these challenges, India's approach of creating and deploying all-women's units to provide more gender-equitable policing has met with a great deal of success.

3 Women at Work

SECURING THE PEACE

Seema and her commanders . . . I'd been a SWAT guy for many years, I've been shot, stabbed, everything. They stood their ground. She said, "If you're fighting, I'm fighting. If they overtake us, I'm staying with you. We don't run." I said, "We can laugh about it in heaven, we can laugh about it in the hospital, or we can stand here in victory on the ground."

Lt. Sal Rodriguez, the coordinator of the UN's formed police units in Liberia at the time of the all-female formed police unit's first deployment

Traditionally, women have been excluded from defending the state and "defined as the protected rather than the protectors, although they have had little control over the conditions of their own protection."[1] However, this tradition is slowly but surely being eroded both locally and globally. As more and more women enter the security field around the world, they are often faced with pressure to legitimize their presence and their right to take up space in the security context. For example, the founder of Securico, now one of Zimbabwe's largest security firms, stated that her gender was among the greatest barriers she faced in setting up her company, since "Obviously, as a woman, people would not believe that I could run a security company."[2] Likewise, the all-female formed police unit (FFPU) has received extensive attention for its community activities, which are also discussed later in this chapter. However, up until now "One thing that has not been properly documented or accounted for has been the actual impact the FPU [formed police unit] is having on security in the county—which is after all their primary function."[3] Thus this chapter first emphasizes that providing security for both the state and human beings is one of the biggest parts, if not the biggest part, of the FFPU's story. "Security" is most often "understood and enacted in a militarized and masculinist way."[4] Recognizing this, and given the special vulnerabilities women face at home and in society, this book applies J. Ann Tickner's feminist perspective in defining security as "the absence of violence, whether it be military, economic, or sexual."[5]

Discussions with the staff of the UN Mission in Liberia (UNMIL) and the Department of Peacekeeping Operations (DPKO) and review of UN documents confirmed that officers of the FFPU do the same security work as their male colleagues in FPUs that are all male or male majority. Members of FFPUs see their work keeping the community secure as their biggest achievement.[6] As one FFPU officer has explained, "People say they feel confident, safe and secure when they see us."[7] Given their many successes in policing, UNMIL's former special representative to the secretary general, Ellen Margrethe Løj, said of the FFPU, "We are first and foremost . . . proud of them being our *best* Formed Police Unit."[8]

Even a current DPKO staffer who was dismissive about FPUs in general ("FPUs are a lesser form of policing") and who adamantly disagreed with the introduction of an all-female unit, favoring gender "integration," admitted, after visiting the FFPU, that "they were impressive." Others agree that the FFPU officers have performed their security tasks impressively. Former DPKO police adviser Mark Kroeker described the Liberian FFPU as "a strong tactical team withstanding the rigors of crowd control and high demands." And the FPU coordinator on the ground when the first FFPU deployed to Liberia said of the group:

> On the first day they arrived and were unpacking we had a major riot. I called the Jordanian and Nigerian FPUs. The Nepalese had trouble getting across town. They started fighting the crowd. My two commissioners showed up, and I said, "You need to leave my area of operation. I don't want a hostage situation. You're going to agitate the crowd more." Then here comes the rock throwing. I called Seema [FFPU commander], and she said, "How many do you need?" I said thirty. She showed up with fifty ready to go and they provided the perimeter security. Most FPUs [which were mostly if not entirely male] would chase them [the rioters], and the Jordanians did that. All the others did. But when they came from behind, the Indians

[women of the FFPU] let them have it. They started throwing smoke gre-
nades. They did such a good job of controlling the crowd. No one got hurt,
and it sent a message that if you want to play silly games we're a lot better at
it than you.

In further showing his respect for the FFPU commanders and officers
and their strength and capacity for protection, he stated, "They'll put a
bullet in you if they need to." This is interesting because the FFPU tend to
try to avoid such engagements more than their fellow FPUs do. Indeed,
the original commanders of the FFPU went out of their way to purpose-
fully request more nonlethal weapons, which they favored relying on in
operations. One commander noted in an interview that her unit had bor-
rowed certain nonlethal equipment from another domestic Indian group,
the Rapid Action Force, to take to Liberia. As she explained, "We have tear
gas solutions and a lot of things, which are really needed, are really effective in order to patrol a mob. So earlier the unit, which had gone to Kosovo,
they had not taken such kind of equipment, but we took along with us the
less lethal sort of weapons . . . tear gas solutions and other things and body
protectors and other things for the requirement of female [officers]."

So there do appear to be some differences in the way the FFPU works.
But although the women of the FFPU are working as women and sometimes for women they are not necessarily in gender-specific roles—indeed,
they usually are not. While they participate in a whole range of extracurricular or "second shift" jobs, as discussed later, security is their main job.
This of course also has important impacts for local women, since "Violence
is a barrier to women's participation in postconflict peace building, perpetuated by women's absence from decision making about political and
economic reconstruction."9

Although India is credited with having the world's first all-female policing units, many other countries have used all-women's police stations or
units to some degree, including Pakistan, Brazil, Kenya, South Africa, the
Philippines, Colombia, Peru, Nicaragua, Ecuador, and Uruguay.10 The reasons for creating women's police stations and the activities they undertake
differ a great deal and link closely to specific local, regional, national, and
sociocultural processes.11 The all-women police forces vary in the ways they
are employed in various countries' contexts, including the degree to which
they specialize in gender-based crimes.12 Sarah Hautzinger explains that

women's police stations have seen three unique types of gender difference in practice: policing solely by female officers, policing that is available only to women citizens, and policing that specializes in gender-based violence, along with structural adaptations to the police organization to allow such a concentration. All of these types link in unique ways to the broader issues, advantages, and disadvantages encountered in specialization and gender segregation.[13]

Research on other gendered policing initiatives shows that the FFPU shares some similarities with approaches taken in other contexts, but it also has some unique characteristics. South Africa's all-women motorcycle police squad may be the closest to the FFPU, as the focus is not on gendered crimes and as the women police are seen as positive role models who can empower women through their work. They prevent crimes and protect VIPs and are noted for their quick response times due to motorcycles' maneuverability in traffic.[14]

Outside India, scholars focusing on Latin American domestic initiatives have conducted the most in-depth research on gendered policing.[15] Hautzinger has engaged in deep exploration of Brazil's first women's police stations, or *delegacias da mulher* (DMs), which opened in 1985. Pointing to examples from her work in Brazil—and noting the all-women police stations in India—where governments have chosen to consolidate all three features of gendered policing, Hautzinger suggests that this "triple cocktail" of "serving women citizens, staffing with women police, and institutional compartmentalization" has brought more value than consternation.[16] Hautzinger explains that while the DMs do have quite limited capacity, and while some women officers in the DMs may hold unhelpful attitudes, in general the DMs can be seen as quite successful because they are widely recognized, many women (over four million between 1985 and 2004) go to them to request help, and just the presence of the DMs has enabled some women to benefit from them even if they do not access them directly (for example, some women have been able to stop spousal abuse they had endured by threatening to report their male partners to DMs).[17]

Sally Engle Merry's work suggests that implementing such frameworks may be fundamental to ensuring that women develop a consciousness about their rights.[18] At the same time, the development of "rights consciousness" and the ability and willingness to claim such rights may depend on the presence of security structures and processes offering reliable support.[19] Likewise, Hautzinger highlights that women dealing with conflict (which they may or may not take to the police) are not inherently winners or losers, victims or victors: each woman's outcome depends upon the security resources she can access and how she perceives her chances of success if she chooses to use them.[20]

Ensuring women's rights to live in situations characterized by peace and security, and to participate themselves in all aspects of peace and security are two separate but often strongly related goals that have broader implications. As Shannon Drysdale Walsh argues, practicing one's rights to participate in democracy may be unimaginable when one is facing fears of violence at home or in public. Hence, "When the state [and here I would add the international community] systemically fails to protect women from violence, it truncates their potential to engage fully in political citizenship."[21] Better addressing women's rights to security can exponentially increase their ability to exercise other rights more broadly.

THE STRONG PROTECTORS

The discursive impacts of the FFPU may also be significant. As Mark Goodale and Sally Engle Merry propose, such practices may have the potential for transforming the way rights are understood.[22] Calls for women's participation in peacekeeping often essentialize women as possessing "feminine" characteristics such as peacefulness and empathy, but the FFPU's actual training includes "shooting, assaulting, and marching exercises" and antiriot tactics.[23] Significantly, from Indian press reports surrounding the deployment of the first FFPU, it appears that the discourse about it may play an important role in reshaping attitudes around the role of women in peace and security by showing that women can successfully participate in traditionally masculine spheres and by emphasizing that femininity can include strength and the capacity for protection.[24]

In media discourse on the topic by far the most common construction of the FFPU has relied on images of its members as strong, competent protectors. Media reports, including reporters' commentaries as well as quotes from members of the Indian FFPU and other UN and Indian government officials, have described the all-female force as a group and as individuals in ways that contrast with traditional, stereotypical understandings of women. The women are portrayed as a strong and well-trained group. Indeed, they are referred to as the "first ever all-women *fighting* contingent," including "103 *female fighting force* and a few male *supporting staff*."[25] Consider what it means for a group of security sector personnel to include women as "*fighters*" and men as "*supporting staff*." It certainly appears to undermine the dominant existing notions of gender roles in international peace and security.

The broader body from which the women are drawn, the Central Reserve Police Force, is "the world's largest para-military force," through which these women "have been providing support . . . in counterinsurgency operations for nearly a decade now and conduct independent cordon and search operations."[26] The FFPU has been variously described as trained in "riot control, firing and unarmed combat"; as having "endurance [and] advanced unarmed combat tactics"; and as being familiar with "crowd and mob control, modern sophisticated weapons, counter-insurgency operations and disaster management."[27]

In the context of their international deployment, the women of the FFPU have been described as "police-soldiers" who wear "combat fatigues" and are "better armed than a regular unit"; their major tasks "includ[e] protecting UN officials and civilian police as they perform their duties."[28] In 2008 Seema Dhundia, the commander of the group, was described as "a master in martial arts and combat weaponry," qualifications that enabled her to lead her "soldiers" to "control riots, patrol the capital Monrovia, and tackle armed robberies and mob violence."[29] Reports explained that "an elite squad of these AK-47 totting [*sic*] women personnel keep a round-the-clock vigil on the office of the President which also houses the West African nation's foreign affairs department in capital Monrovia" and said they were maintaining law and order and combating violence.[30] Further reports claimed that they had "disarmed more than one lakh [one hundred thousand] of ex-combatants, supported the country's first democratic elections in decades and provided the security necessary for reconstruction and economic development."[31] Moreover, reporters lauded the group for playing "pro-active" roles "in quelling riots and breaking drug rings," thereby "giv[ing] Liberia the strength to come out from the shadow of the UN peace-keeping forces and strengthen its own Liberian National Police by inducting women."[32] As the group with the "muscle," the women could also "respond to calls for armed back-up from the national police who, unlike the Indian unit, do not carry arms."[33]

The media statements of battalion commander Dhundia directly counter portrayals of women as lacking skills and authority, particularly in traditionally male-dominated occupations. In one article she stated: "We're prepared to take casualties. My girls know the hazards of the call of duty—they have to do it, they're soldiers."[34] Elsewhere she stated that the contingent had been "carved out from a paramilitary force," that "as far as training is concerned, it is almost on the same line of what army recruits get, and that they would carry out their work "with utmost professionalism."[35] Dhundia situated herself as a protector among protectors: "My aim was to keep my troops safe and also to live up to the expectations of the UN, my own organisation and the Liberians too."[36]

Other UN officials have similarly emphasized the leadership, authority, competence, and strength of the female police officers and have been careful to describe them, not as somehow "different" from other women, but as exemplifying what women can do. For instance, Løj, the UN special representative to the secretary general for Liberia, commented that "the unit hit the ground running on arrival and showed itself a capable force, protecting UN officials and VIPs, as well as protecting various installations." Løj further commended "the superb professional performance of the first batch of female Indian police peacekeepers" in fulfilling essential roles, including helping to "deal with possible civil unrest such as violent demonstrations and communal tensions."[37]

Løj and some other UN officials were careful to emphasize the potential cooperation and similarities between FFPU members and local Liberian women. Løj stated that the Indian women not only had helped to make the streets of Monrovia safer but had set "a shining example for the women and girls of Liberia . . . [, motivating] more Liberian women to become police officers" and launching a joint UN–Liberia campaign against rape.[38] The campaign thus offered a construction that embraced collaboration and input from local women. Andrew Hughes, a UN DPKO police adviser, reported that, "to have strong, confident and capable women police officers in that environment sends all the right messages. If these women can do it . . . then why can't women who are in this society do the same thing? The answer is . . . they can and they should."[39] Others described the FFPU's presence as an "encouragement for Liberian women to come forward, and help rebuild their country by participating in the forces of law and order."[40]

Indian officials have placed FFPUs in the larger context of women's crucial role in establishing peace. Hardeep Singh Puri, permanent representative of India to the UN, for example, praised the FFPU initiative on the grounds that "greater participation of women in areas of conflict prevention, peace negotiations, peacekeeping and post conflict reconstruction is the sine qua non for lasting peace and security."[41] Indian leaders have also challenged prevailing norms by situating the women as strong protectors, in contrast to traditional notions of women as victims needing protection. Lt. Gen. Randhir Kumar Mehta remarked, "They are not just tokens but operationally proven. . . You know, in our legends, the male deities are occasionally defeated, but the female deities never are."[42] Comments have tended to link the FFPU's advancement of gender equality to its capable performance in the field: "Though a new beginning for gender equality in peacekeeping, this deployment is a continuation of India's consistent commitment to peacekeeping operations. . . It is about performance. You have all performed your duties well and met our high expectations."[43]

The representation of the FFPU in the Indian media suggests a need to broaden the feminist analysis of women's participation as peacekeepers beyond short-term material outcomes. Such participation may also have longer-term impacts through shifts in the discourse that challenge gender norms regarding peace and security. The introduction of the FFPU is a significant step, both in ensuring that women are directly engaged in such processes and in shifting gendered discourses of peace and security.

THE UN'S APPRAISAL OF THE FFPU

The UN has touted the Indian unit in Liberia as a role model for women's involvement in security, leading to greater numbers of women joining the Liberian national police force.[44] A UNMIL 2010 study looking at the FFPU alongside other (predominantly male) FPUs from Nepal, Nigeria, and Jordan, found that the women in the FFPU viewed their mission more broadly. While the all-male FPU saw their outcomes in terms of reducing crime rates for armed robbery and assault, they paid little attention to the wider provision of human security.[45] In contrast, FFPU members were encouraged, by unit and mission leaders, to develop an enhanced sense of contribution, including through developing outreach activities to the local population. This led to their having a broader outlook compared to their male colleagues—including greater attention to human security and using resources in innovative ways to improve the security situation.[46] The FFPU members were strongly motivated, not only to provide safety, but to serve as role models; though facing their own challenges, they could see how their work affected women and girls and thus felt a "a strong sense of personal responsibility for continuing this trend."[47]

The UNMIL report highlighted the FFPU as an example of best practice.[48] It noted that according to community members in the area where the FFPU was stationed, women peacekeepers had enhanced security through their armed presence and through such practices as lighting systems and night patrols.[49] One focus group member stated, "Their presence is our safety."[50] In addition to effectively providing security for government buildings and for people, the FFPU seems to have effectively modeled women's ability to do police work for the Liberian population: their presence has correlated with the rise of the percentage of women in Liberia's national police force.[51]

POLICING OF SEXUAL AND GENDER-BASED VIOLENCE

UNMIL states that the FFPU has acted as a UN resource in combating sexual violence, and the Liberian community has cited the FFPU as providing both deterrent and response mechanisms.[52] Research has likewise found that the FFPU has reduced the rate of sexual harassment and rape in Liberia,[53] and another researcher adds that since the FFPU arrived sexual abuse and exploitation rates in the area have plummeted.[54] Furthermore, a DPKO gender affairs associate has noted that when these crimes do occur under the FFPU's watch, the FFPU officers, by their presence alone, appear to "encourage Liberian women to report instances of sexual violence."[55] Increased reporting of sexual and gender-based violence may in itself indicate confidence in the security sector, which can be understood as a significant move toward security for women.[56]

Many commentators have attributed the FFPU's enhanced responsiveness to crimes of sexual and gender-based violence to "natural" qualities of women. For example, one female officer is reported as saying that "with peacekeeping contingents frequently facing allegations of sexual abuse and exploitation, the presence of women *naturally* inspires confidence."[57] Løj, the UN special envoy, echoed such views in her official statements, suggesting that Indian policewomen had "infused a culture of tolerance, a tradition of respect and a *natural inclination towards peaceful co-existence* in UN operations."[58] Likewise, the FFPU commander understood the special capacity of her unit to reside in their natural ability to relate to people, especially women and other mothers: "What mattered, perhaps, was that *we were caring and knew how to behave* and were thus able to generate more confidence among the local people than men. The Liberian women didn't hesitate to come to us since *we understood their issues as well as that of the children*."[59] Others commented that women had special abilities to relate to people, particularly women, so they "expected that victims would find it easier to confide in female officers."[60]

Representing the FPPU women as mothers positioned them as able to relate to other mothers and children. Not only is motherhood associated with making sacrifices, but evoking such images of domesticity may legitimize women's public roles by challenging the public/private divide.[61] Indeed, women around the world have often drawn on their respected status as mothers to gain political leverage.[62] In this sense, motherhood can be understood as malleable, resilient, complicated, and contingent.[63] While mobilizing motherhood in radical and innovative ways, women's groups centered on their status as mothers have rarely been able to destabilize dominant views.[64] However, by drawing on their status as mothers while taking on other roles that contradict traditional expectations, the Indian women of the FFPU may be perceived in unique ways that destabilize dominant assumptions.

While recognizing these possibilities, it is important to critically engage with the existing framework, which assumes that, because of experience in "mothering," women (of the FFPU and in general) can "naturally" deal with crimes against women, including conflict-related sexual and gender-based violence. For one thing, most, but not all, women in the FFPU are mothers. Motherhood is not a "natural" state for every woman everywhere. Second, when women are mothers and draw on that experience in positive ways in their work, this ought to be recognized as a skill developed through relevant experience in empathetic and appropriate responses, rather than an innate trait. Likewise, the FFPU's capacity for dealing with sexual and gender-based violence is probably evident, not because "women are inherently better at dealing with the emotional aspects of conflict, but because it is more socially acceptable for women to do so and less acceptable for men, especially male soldiers."[65] Moreover, as Robert Rubinstein notes, the way an individual peacekeeper will respond to a challenge depends on the training he or she receives; the social environment in which he or she operates, and the personal motivation he or she carries into the situation.[66] All of these must thus be considered in approaching new innovations in peacekeeping practice and policy.

Assuming that women peacekeepers can "naturally" handle such important and serious crimes may leave both them and the communities they serve underprepared and lacking in appropriate training, resources, and strategies. After all, just like men, women peacekeepers need adequate and appropriate training for doing all aspects of their job, including responding to crimes against women. Because security work has not traditionally been seen as natural for women, much of the discourse around the FFPU has focused on how *well trained* the officers have been to do their job of providing security fully and well. Yet because it is often erroneously assumed that women somehow, as if by instinct, know how to deal with things like sexual and gender-based violence, policewomen in the FFPU have often been left to fend for themselves in learning how to respond to such crimes.

Hautzinger has documented a similar situation in her research on Brazil's women's police stations, where she noted it was hit-or-miss as to whether women police received training on dealing with violence against women. Most women officers had no qualifications or training relevant to being "women's police" other than being women themselves.[67] Some policewomen working in women's police stations at times acted in dehumanizing, distancing, and authoritative ways as compared to crisis center staff, who related to the victims in ways that were more cooperative, nonjudgmental, and intimate. Again, this was probably because crisis center workers had actually been *trained* to deal with gender-based violence, rather than being assumed to have expertise in the area merely by virtue of being female.[68] Moreover, Hautzinger suggests that policewomen's strong identification with being police and thus to some extent masculinized, potentially violent workers could impede their capacity for identifying with the female victims of crime requiring their assistance.[69] After all, research suggests that both women and men police are more accepting of the need for regular, official violence than are their civilian counterparts.[70] When policewomen in Brazil received training on gender-based violence, they tended to have a stronger sense of purpose and heightened resolve; however, most of the time such education and training was unavailable, exacerbating the resentment and alienation many policewomen faced.[71] Overall, Hautzinger found that the assumption that women would do policing differently just by virtue of being women was not supported. Women did policing differently only when they received "specialized training about violence and gender dynamics."[72]

The Liberian National Police seeks to recruit more women in order to improve responsiveness to sexual and gender-based violence. "The idea is that women will be more likely to view crimes through a gendered lens and be better at investigating gender related crimes (women are better suited to interview female victims)."[73] But although they have relied on narratives of women's "natural" abilities, they also have taken the important step of recognizing the need for providing female recruits with adequate training in such cases. A similarly contradictory approach to women's recruitment has come up again and again in policing organizations around the world.

Throughout the interviews for this book, training kept coming up again and again as a crucial element. As one previous FFPU commander had to say:

> I insist on this issue, [this] point that they must be fully well trained, fully equipped. . . . [Whether one is] a male peacekeeper or a female peacekeeper, the training has to be good. Training, the sensitization, the acclimatization, this thing has to be good. Because if you have a female peacekeeper who is not trained properly . . . and who is not able to handle her equipment properly, who is not aware of the environment, what is happening around her, so there is no need. . . . What is the point of having a female peacekeeper there

if she's not trained? So training is the most important thing, whether the peacekeepers are female or male, the training has to be really good. The peacekeepers are really [needing] to be properly sensitized. If they are not, they will be a failure.

Specifically regarding gender-based crimes, she went on to say, "You can't deny the fact that having a female peacekeeper will definitely lower the [incidence of] gender-based crimes. Definitely, it will come down, but that female peacekeeper has to be trained properly. Because if she's not trained, then she's of no use. Even . . . a male peacekeeper, if he's not properly trained, he's of no use."

Later contingents of the FFPU benefited from this emphasis on training that the first commander had made a cornerstone of the FFPU's work from the beginning. As one later commander said, when her contingent arrived, they could take advantage of training that had already been designed for those that had come before and that was now in place for her use. "So what we do is, we just augment it. We just talk to the predecessor: 'Is there something else that you need to include in this?' If they tell you, 'Yes, this is what we are facing right now, maybe this is something we should include,' we would just incorporate it into the curriculum and we would go ahead."

In this way the first FFPU has made serious contributions to sustainable, well-developed, and adaptive training practices for both traditional law-and-order security and issues like sexual and gender-based violence. Overall, the FFPU's responsiveness to dealing with such cases was based not on "natural" abilities but on knowledge obtained by the first commander's initiative to ensure that officers would receive special training on this issue. Since it had been assumed that female police could naturally undertake such duties, even though they had been trained only in traditional security such as riot control, FFPU officers were left with the responsibility to seek training for themselves and the rest of the contingent. They should be commended for doing so. At the same time, their example should serve as a reminder that all peacekeepers, both male and female, need to be properly trained in *all* aspects of security for *all* people, not just traditional law-and-order activities that focus on protecting a male subject as the default citizen.[74]

Moreover, it is important to avoid framing the issue in terms of the need for women to solve "women's problems" of conflict-related sexual and gender-based violence, as opposed to recognizing the broader gender norms that contribute to the issue and the persistent reluctance or inability of men or masculine institutions such as peacekeeping organizations to sufficiently address it. As noted earlier, women often state they would prefer to report crimes to female police, but it is important to recognize that this preference may be partly due to female police's better training around crimes committed against women. At the same time, Kyle Beardsley and colleagues report that evidence from their study in Liberia "suggests that training can make police more attuned to SGBV [sexual and gender-based violence] regardless of a police officer's sex."[75] Thus it is necessary to ensure that male officers receive appropriate training and have the chance to develop more empathetic attitudes around working with women, rather than expecting women to take on full responsibility for a "double shift" involving both traditional security work and to respond specifically to crimes commonly deemed "women's issues." It is also important to ensure that women officers are not pigeonholed into working solely with particular crimes against women, given that they may contribute to achieving a much broader range of peace and security goals. After all, women cannot solve these issues alone. It is crucial to remember that "violence against women is a men's issue"[76] and an issue for institutions designed by and run by men, including the UN.

While facing many challenges to their legitimacy as peacekeepers due to their being women or their working in an all-female unit, the FFPU have clearly done a great deal to break down barriers to women's participation in peacekeeping in particular and peace and security in general. Through their actions and public recognition for them, the FFPU have shown that women, including those working in women-only units, can meet and exceed expectations around providing security, whether in traditional law-and-order policing or in dealing with gender-based crimes. This is important for advancing the interests of women who may wish to take on careers as peacekeepers, for women in postconflict zones, and for women who may wish to have the option of reporting to female security personnel. The FFPU women's presence is also significant in its capacity for disrupting widely accepted narratives that pressure men and boys to participate in violence in order to "prove" their manhood and that marginalize the participation of women in peace processes by limiting what roles are perceived to be "appropriate" or "natural" for women. *This is a direct challenge to discourses that represent women as victims in need of protection.*

At the same time, it is clear that the FFPU and women in peace and security in general have to contend with stereotypes that have emerged from false assumptions that women inherently possess the skills and abilities needed to provide adequate protection and security for other women. This must be and has been challenged by the hard work of the FFPU commanders in ensuring their recruits are well trained across the board. In acting as well-trained, capable security providers who also make space for the use of non-lethal options and training that include attention to care for victims of crime, the FFPU may unsettle existing dominant discourses around gender and peacekeeping. After all, they show that self-proclaimed girls and mothers can create secure environments as effectively as men, and perhaps at times even more effectively. Likewise, the presence of the FFPU may challenge binary views of masculinity and femininity, highlighting a need to (a) critically reflect on expectations of both male and female peacekeepers and how these may be shaped by gender norms in ways that hinder the provision of security; (b) ensure adequate training; and (c) support women working in peacekeeping, including acknowledging their capacity for making significant and crucial contributions to provision of security.

4 Political Economy, Women, and Peacekeeping

There [are] also stories wherein the women come from very, very poor backgrounds in the villages, so obviously it is an opportunity for them . . . for the women, the ranks. So having passed the tenth standard, you were getting into a central government job, which is supposed to be a very prestigious central government job having just got out of school. . . . You are able to support your family. You are considered a kind of an empowered person back in the village or where you come from. You win some kind of an influence over the society. You're independent. You're learning.

Former FFPU commander

A number of feminist scholars have argued that international actors are complicit in creating local and global economies and thus that there is a need for integrating politics, security, and economics.[1] Specifically, they emphasize that security and political economy are intimately related and gendered in form and function.[2] J. Ann Tickner notes that women experience particular economic vulnerabilities at home, at work, and in broad practices of subsistence, since women often perform unpaid care labor, which is valued less, leading to economic and consequently social inequality for women.[3] Not only are women expected to do informal, unpaid work outside the workplace, but in most parts of the world they are paid less money than men for performing the same work.[4] In this way, gender hierarchies affect women's economic status and create social structures that disadvantage women.[5]

Feminist scholars of international relations have thus suggested that access to resources is crucial for women's capacity to participate in decision making and to reduce their relative vulnerability to violence.[6] This is a view shared by human security theorists, who claim that economic security—or access to the resources necessary to provide for oneself and one's family—is a key component of security; hence, people lacking economic security are by definition insecure.[7] At the same time, effectively reforming the security sector, including through police capacity building, is key for sustainable economic development.[8] Overall, as Cynthia Enloe puts it, "A woman's economic independence and her physical health, security, and autonomy are mutually interdependent: curtail one, and you curtail the likelihood of the other."[9]

Researchers have therefore argued that opportunities for overcoming economic disadvantage may reduce women's vulnerability to violence. For example, Jacqui True suggests that "it is the gendered social and economic inequalities between women and men that make women more vulnerable to violence and abuse in whatever context. . . . It is women's impoverished situation relative to men that is at the root of violence."[10] Economic empowerment is likewise a major factor in addressing gender-based violence that disproportionately affects women and girls. Following True, economic empowerment here is interpreted as "improving women's socioeconomic and legal status. This would include increasing women's awareness of their rights and establishing measures to ensure women's rights related to owning and disposing of property and assets. Enabling women and girls' access to secondary and tertiary education and to decent employment with good working conditions and remuneration should also be an integral part of antiviolence strategies."[11]

In general, the UN's Women, Peace and Security (WPS) agenda has failed to incorporate such views of security, explicitly omitting political economic aspects and rejecting the notion that "there can be no meaningful distinction between economic policy and social policy."[12] This is despite scholars' claim that Resolution 1325 has been so inconsistently and sparsely implemented not only because of a lack of political will but also because of inadequate funding of UN Women, which, along with the Department of Peacekeeping Operations, is charged with its implementation.[13] This is an issue for international initiatives aimed at improving women's lives more broadly. As Natalie Hudson and Anne Marie Goetz note, "There are still major problems. UN Women now has the power tools but no electricity . . . We have had enormous difficulty raising money. Yet we have a massive mandate—to advance women's rights everywhere in the world."[14]

However, calls for incorporating a political economic analysis in efforts at pursuing gender equity in peace and security initiatives may be gaining greater traction in recent years. Resolution 1889 (2009) of the WPS agenda was "the first to include language that encourages member states to address the socioeconomic needs of women."[15] Despite this exception, most WPS work has discussed increasing women's participation in peacekeeping with little or no attention to what that would entail or to what costs women incur when they do participate.

Noting this, I am interested in whether and how the presence and practice of the FFPU might facilitate economic empowerment for women, particularly by providing decent employment with comparatively high pay—which can play an important role in global antiviolence strategies seeking to empower women and girls. After all, globally women's participation in the labor force has increased, yet the gender wage gap remains. Traditionally male occupations like policing and peacekeeping may be one possible breakthrough area. Investigating how more women might become employed in these occupations can contribute to the ongoing and significant political project of increasing women's access to security and justice as well as more broadly to social, political, and economic empowerment. Still, critical engagement is needed; it is not sufficient to assume that women taking on work in traditionally male-dominated roles will receive adequate pay to improve their circumstances. Indeed, research on Brazil's all-women police stations has found that the low salaries women police received meant they often had to take on second jobs to generate necessary income for survival.[16] Research has also noted that in some instances women's greater economic independence has been linked with more exposure to physical and/or structural violence.[17]

In considering what, if any gains, women working as peacekeepers might access, it is also necessary to deconstruct existing gender dichotomies that marginalize women in security institutions and to consider whether and to what degree women peacekeepers serving on missions are also expected to do the informal, unpaid care work many women perform at home. Looking at the FFPU provides a chance to consider what duties are expected of women in policing, particularly in peacekeeping, what duties they are doing, and what drives them.

THE FFPU THROUGH A POLITICAL ECONOMIC LENS

While peacekeeping is most often discussed in terms of how peacekeepers can provide a valuable service to the postconflict areas where they are deployed, Kathleen Jennings makes the compelling point that "peacekeeping practitioners and policymakers need to pay more attention to the question of whom peacekeeping is for—acknowledging in doing so that peacekeepers themselves are also beneficiaries."[18] Working in policing in general or as peacekeepers in particular can be a valuable opportunity for women, possibly increasing their status and access to rights and decision making.

Looking more deeply at how and why women get involved in policing and what barriers they face is important. It appears that women working in the FFPU or in security sector roles more broadly often take on unexpected, nontraditional positions in their home and work lives. This may be facilitated through the financial contribution they are able to make because of the economic benefits they receive from this work. Indeed, as will be discussed, research has shown that higher pay is precisely the reason many women in India joined the police. Overall, enhanced access to security sector work may significantly advance women's economic empowerment, a key factor in achieving sustainable peace.

Research suggests that initiatives mandating women's participation in traditionally male-dominated activities have delivered important results. In a randomized field experiment, Andrew Beath, Christia Fotini, and Ruben Enikolopov conducted surveys with thirteen thousand female and male respondents in five hundred Afghan villages to explore whether the use of gender quotas in development programs might affect women's political, economic, and social status. They found that even in what they described as a "highly conservative context" such initiatives improved outcomes around women's participation in some political, economic, and social activities. [19] They documented gains in support for women's participation in village decision making and governance.[20] They also found that women in the villages that experienced the quota program generated more income, were more likely to have assets, and enjoyed expanded mobility.[21] They did not, however, find any effects on women's position in the family, role in family decision making, or control over the income or assets that women identified as their own. Nor did they find any changes in views about women's position in society more broadly.

But a qualitative study by Naila Kabeer, Ayesha Khan, and Naysan Adlparvar that followed twelve women in Afghanistan who had gained access to microfinance loans found evidence that making a strong contribution to household income could in fact improve women's status within the household.[22] In particular, some women—through bringing loans into the household—gained increased voice and influence there. Several spoke of reductions in domestic violence following the relaxing of economic pressures on men as the primary household providers, and many felt they were accorded greater respect both in their families and in their local communities.[23] Several women also reported expanded social interaction.[24] The authors argue that since women's material dependence can make them vulnerable to attacks if they question the existing social order and constraints on women within it, women may require some level of economic independence in order to claim their rights.[25]

Although Beath and colleagues' study of the impact of gender quotas found less far-reaching effects, their study was a short-term one looking at an area that had only in the previous two years experienced a program using gender quotas.[26] Long-term outcomes may well reveal measurable changes around attitudes on women's roles in family decision-making or in wider society. The authors note that other research in the same context has found that exposure to women leaders at the local level has led to long-term change through greater acceptance of women's political leadership, as shown by their chances of reelection and women's and men's views on female leadership aptitude.[27] Long-term effects of programs using quotas suggest that widespread changes to social attitudes could require more long-term experience with women in these new roles. On this basis, they suggest that development interventions such as gender quotas for women's participation "could arguably prove to be . . . promising . . . for other gender-biased environments across the world."[28]

At the same time, as Enloe convincingly argues, "It takes resources and access to be 'heard' when and where it matters. Consequently, those who reside at the margins tend to be deemed 'silent.'"[29] Thus, as Maha Muna notes, "It remains important to ask *which* women are included."[30] Certainly the women who have commanded FFPUs have been able to voice their perspectives in the media and gain a great deal of public attention. This reflects the broader research finding that militaries and military leaders often have significant influence regarding state priorities and policies,[31] and the same can be said of police services and police leaders. More significantly, there are prospects for the "rank and file" women of the IPS, the CRPF, and the FFPU to gain more of a voice politically and socially.

Capacity to participate in many peacebuilding and security initiatives is strongly tied to economic status, with participation being mostly the preserve of elite women. Yet participation in well-paid policing and peacekeeping jobs is open to working-class women. As such, work in the FFPU provides opportunities for their economic empowerment.[32] The initiative thus diverges from international policy making that, although aiming to empower women politically and economically, typically caters to a narrow portion of urban, young, middle-class professionals while doing little if anything for ordinary women.[33]

Which women participate in peacekeeping is also shaped by the international relations of states, including economic disparities. For example, states that are poor benefit from sending troops and receiving a fixed rate of compensation from the UN, which also provides training.[34] Richer countries tend to pay for missions while sending few if any troops, while developing states provide the greatest portion of peacekeepers.[35] Countries that contribute the most peacekeepers are often motivated by financial incentives, though these vary by troop-contributing country and peacekeeping roles.[36] This is significant for the Indian women of the FFPU because they operate as a formed unit deployed and overseen by India, rather than as individual officers recruited into UNPOL. Those employed by the UN as individual officers receive US$100 assistance for daily living expenses, while those in FPUs are the deploying country's responsibility and receive $1.28 daily.[37] What implications this may have for intersections of gender and other factors in this context is unclear, but it certainly suggests the need for further economic analysis of what FFPUs mean for women who participate in them as personnel, rather than working in mixed-gender environments as individual officers.

Overall, it appears that FFPU officers' enhanced economic status may open new opportunities for them at home and in the public realm, as others in both spheres may be more open to hearing them when they have access to greater resources. Indeed, the political economy of the role they take on may provide enhanced bargaining power. After all, "no groups are more 'up' than" the international actors responsible for peace and security, and they work in powerful institutions.[38]

This access to resources and status is a significant motivation for many women to join the security sector and to take part in peacekeeping. One study that examined motivations for joining the Indian Police Service, though it did not disaggregate by sex or say how many, if any, women were included in the survey or whether their motivations differed from those of male recruits, found that the top career drivers were, in order, meaning (contributing to something worthwhile), expertise (gaining mastery of a specialized field with skills, knowledge, and capacity), and status (being admired, recognized, and respected by the wider community).[39] Another study on all-women's police stations in India did find one woman working as a police officer who "stated that she was from a village that had a substantial area known for violence, and she wanted to help reduce violence and help women,"[40] but this was the exception rather than the rule. Most of the women police came from families of police. These women may have seen the police as something familiar to them personally, despite its being a male-dominated occupation in general. At the same time, the study found that some women had entered policing specifically because the salary would enable them to help their family,[41] and it is possible that the higher earnings might offer at least some of them options for being more empowered in family decision making. Similar themes came up in this research on the FFPU.

In her work on women in militaries, Mathers argues that motivations for joining may be as varied as the women who join and as diverse as those of men who join, but she emphasizes that often, "in both rich and poor nations, women's primary motivation is economic."[42] It appears that the same may hold true for women choosing to join domestic and international police units. When asked why they had joined the police service or decided to take part in a peacekeeping mission, the main reasons the FFPU officers listed concerned the pursuit of meaning, money, and opportunity—similar to the reasons for joining reported by other police officers in India. As a former commander of the FFPU had to say on the topic:

> So getting an opportunity to [go] on a very prestigious mission was ... a lifetime opportunity for them to step out, see something new, work with a set of whole new ... different cultures, various countries, troops coming from all over the world. ... I think they come back to the same rank. They more or less come back to the same battalion that they were serving in. I think whatever you go with the, in the United Nations, it's a huge bonus. ... And then you have your additional salary, which is coming in India. Isn't that a bonus? It's a great bonus. ... Once you are there, I think most important is the confidence that you gain and exposure to a totally different working atmosphere.

THE SECOND SHIFT OF WOMEN PEACEKEEPERS

While women peacekeepers of the FFPU can access higher wages and the associated social status, they must invest more time in their work than their male colleagues do, or even probably those women deployed in mixed-gender contingents. In addition to providing traditional security in numerous ways outlined in the previous chapter and in line with their male colleagues in the same missions, the FFPU do extensive volunteer work in the community where they are deployed. From the UN perspective, in which policy makers are "driven to produce value for money in programming and to produce tangible, measurable results," such "extra output" from women may be lauded as representing "value for money."[43] As Kristen Cordell notes, "unlike their male counterparts," the FFPU "devote their personal time and resources to interacting with the community," including working with schools and orphanages, providing food and clean water in areas near schools, offering free health care services for pregnant women and people who have contracted malaria, and running a community summer camp that teaches classic Indian dance, self-defense, and first aid to Liberian school-girls.[44] As Carole Doucet, UN gender adviser in Liberia, for example, noted, "Where we found a difference [between male and female peacekeepers] is in their perceptions of their role. ... The women see themselves as more broadly involved in the community."[45]

Louise Olsson, Anita Schjølset, and Frida Möller argue that research needs to explore whether gendered divisions of labor exist in international peace operations.[46] Thus they suggest the need to use both quantitative data on women's participation and qualitative data on policies around women's involvement, recruitment methods, and retention efforts.[47] To this I would add that it is crucial to ask what the women do where they are deployed, what they are expected to do, and how their presence has been justified, as these all are likely to have significant influence on current and future participation by women. When these questions are asked in the context of the FFPU, the women's "second shift" becomes evident.

Many female officers in the FFPU cited some benefits of the extra efforts they had made to improve the lives of women, even when this was an added, gendered expectation of them as women.[48] As one former FFPU commander explained: "It also helps us in doing better, putting our best in the Mission field, knowing in the back of our minds that we are being presented . . . as an inspirational role for the Liberian women. . . . You deliberately try to outshine . . . your own capacities."

However, as previously noted, the idea of working "as women for women" did not come up when women were asked why they had joined the police service or decided to take part in a peacekeeping mission. Nor is it part of the standard expectations for a (traditionally male) peacekeeper. Hence I argue here that this work constitutes a "second shift" for women peacekeepers. Moreover, it appears to stem, not from a "natural" commitment or disposition for helping other women, but from differing social expectations for women peacekeepers.

Women peacekeepers tend to take on missions for pragmatic reasons. Those who enter FFPUs, in contrast to women who deploy as a small minority in male-majority contingents, may be more able to perform the security roles they signed on for, while being allowed to "keep" their femininity, since it is not seen as a distraction in a women-only unit, and certain displays of femininity in this context are instrumentalized, expected, and naturalized through discourses that serve to legitimize and even demand this second-shift work of women peacekeepers.

In the short term, local populations may benefit from this work. However, constantly expecting women police to take on a second shift may actually perpetuate gendered differences in access to security. In analyzing women's police stations in Brazil, Sarah Hautzinger encountered many problems that kept officers from achieving the expected outcomes. On the basis of her research, she suggests these problems were due not primarily to the individual policewomen but to problems at the administrative level: adequate resources, both human and material, were not provided to ensure effective functioning of the women's police stations.[49] Women's police stations in Brazil promised many ancillary services, like social work, but given underfunding and a serious lack of psychologists and social workers on staff, this promise only increased the burden put on women police.[50] In short, the officers working in the women's police stations were under-resourced and overworked. As a result, many found their workload overwhelming, some became desensitized or traumatized from hearing repeated stories of violence, and some at times felt unable to effectively prevent, punish, or intervene in offenses.[51] When it comes to women's participation in the security sector, including peacekeeping, "It remains important to ask . . . are we expecting more from women (super heroines) than we expect of men?"[52]

NATURAL SUPERHEROINES (OR SUPERHUMAN RESOURCES) OF PEACEKEEPING?

As noted in the previous chapter, discourse around the FFPU has sought to challenge gender dichotomies and stereotypes that portray women as incapable of providing protection. Yet it can still tend to construct women as naturally peaceful, compassionate, and willing and able to address the needs of other women and children. Although such claims can draw on and perpetuate certain stereotypes of women's traditional roles, Kathleen Jennings suggests this does not make them "necessarily misguided or harmful." She notes that they are often deployed to convey positive messages around women's talents and capacities and that women peacekeepers themselves sometimes point to these qualities while at the same time highlighting their training and professionalism.[53] Nevertheless, she argues, such stereotypes, though flattering, can be problematic and patronizing.[54] This is particularly interesting in light of a study by Liora Sion, which found that (male) peacekeepers tended to see peacekeeping missions as feminine and thus rejected women's participation as a potential threat to their masculinity and prestige.[55] Sion argues that women's participation in peacekeeping takes away the missions' value in proving masculinity.[56] At the same time, many UN departments, especially those associated with military action and/or emergencies, have been seen as "naturally male,"[57] so suggestions that women, too, may be naturally suited to peacekeeping may play a role in unsettling existing gender binaries. That being said, such complicated narratives can create tensions between the divergent identities women soldiers have to (re)negotiate.[58] The same may apply to women peacekeepers in some circumstances.

While there are valid reasons why some women and children may find it easier to communicate with female security personnel, it is important not to assume that female personnel are inherently more suited to such work, and also to avoid constructing local women, often in non-Western, nonindustrialized contexts, as hapless victims in need of protection and lacking agency. As noted in chapter 1, Marsha Henry's analysis of *All Girl Squad,* the BBC documentary on the FFPU, points out how the film sets up this very dichotomy by juxtaposing the FFPU, portrayed as tough, strong, respectable women, with Liberian women, portrayed as damaged victims.[59] Perhaps to avoid the contradictions of women being armed yet "naturally" peaceful, many constructions of the FFPU have relied on labels with connotations of traditional femininity, such as "girls," "ladies," and "mothers," even when those labels are joined with activities including danger or force. Several news reports have used this language.[60]

This assumption that women are naturally suited to peace and to working for women, or the "affirmative essentialist ideal," ignores the possibility that women may gravitate toward military or police careers "for the same pragmatic reasons as many men," such as job security, a decent wage, and the chance to take on challenges.[61] In other words, most of the time women become peacekeepers "not primarily to help other women, but rather to improve their own career prospects or increase their earning potential."[62] Yet assumptions based on the flawed "affirmative essentialist ideal" persist and lead to expectations that women should do extra, unpaid work in peacekeeping. These assumptions have been drawn on, stated, and reified in order to justify women's inclusion in peacekeeping on instrumentalist grounds.

Although women are often devalued politically and economically, the dominant instrumentalist case made for women's inclusion in peacekeeping "sells" women, or more specifically the perceived "natural" abilities and skills of women, as necessary and valuable for the goal of attaining international peace and security. In the case of the FFPUs, framing the need for women's participation in peace and security in instrumentalist terms limits options around whether and how women can demand and access their rights, both within the state and through the state's international contributions. While the introduction of this policy innovation can have important outcomes for women accessing and exercising their rights, the dominance of the instrumentalist discourse denies the crucial need to challenge embedded stereotypes that underscore limitations to women's rights to security in the international sphere more broadly. Likewise, some argue that instrumentalizing women's participation risks deflecting attention from the central problems of inequality.[63]

While a rights-based approach and the instrumentalist approach have both long coexisted, the instrumentalist approach has over time become increasingly dominant in discussions of women's participation in peace and security, particularly in peacekeeping.[64] Reflecting back to 2000, when Resolution 1325 was passed, a UNIFEM official interviewed by Natalie Hudson reported that "instrumental arguments are the only arguments that work with policy-makers. Nobody is interested in women because it is the right thing to do or because it's about human rights—nobody."[65] Anne Marie Goetz, formerly chief adviser to Peace and Security for UN Women, says that while some policy makers are committed to gender equality as a transformative, long-term project, "they also have to write justifications for programs and activities based on instrumentalist arguments about social, peace, economic and environmental pay-offs of gender equality"; this, she says, "can alienate feminist allies" in the struggle.[66]

In discussions of women's participation in peacekeeping specifically, the UN has increasingly focused on a discourse of operational effectiveness,[67] with women's deployment seen as "an operational imperative" that is assumed to "increase the peace."[68] Some scholars and authors outside the UN arguing for women's inclusion in peacekeeping have also taken this approach. They argue for women's inclusion on the basis of operational effectiveness,[69] or they construct women as "untapped resources."[70]

In these arguments, women, as women, are expected to "naturally" do an extraordinarily wide range of important work. Indeed, the UN says that the presence of women can

- help reduce conflict and confrontation
- improve access and support for local women
- empower women in the community
- provide a greater sense of security to local populations, including women and children
- help create a safer and less fearful environment for women
- highlight the UN's commitment to diversity, inclusion and gender equality
- broaden the repertoire of skills and styles available within a peacekeeping mission[71]

The UN has enumerated several other benefits from having a strong presence of women peacekeepers, including creating safer spaces for women and girls who have survived sexual violence, increasing the participation of women in national police forces, enhancing the capacity to calm crowds in riots, and increasing the reporting of sexual violence.[72]

The UN's predilection for an instrumentalist case for women's participation in peacekeeping over potential alternatives, such as rights-based arguments, suggests that the "real goal" of recruiting women is not gender equality but the "more palatable alternative claim" that women make the organization work better yet do not threaten its identity or core functions.[73] Furthermore, under the dominant instrumentalist paradigm at the United Nations, women may be heard only when they are willing and able to take on the "natural superheroine" narrative as their own. A study by Sheri Gibbings, for example, found that women advocating for gender equity at the UN were expected to deliver only uplifting, positive messages in order to prove their "value" as peacemakers and fit into the existing discourse on the Women, Peace and Security agenda. If they failed to do so, "they risked being dismissed entirely."[74] This tendency denies other ways of knowing, being, and doing and therefore constricts the ways women can be heard or can contribute more broadly to important questions before the international community. In this environment women are "being 'marketed', and women's abilities are framed to convince the current decision-makers of the utility of their abilities and knowledge"[75] or to legitimize the institution's practices. Such marketing occurs, for example, to showcase the institution's inclusiveness and democracy, even when, at the same time, women's experiences and perspectives are ignored and women's views, skills, and resources are not fully utilized.[76]

This instrumentalist view's assumptions about women's different "natural" inclinations and abilities can also lead to stereotyping, including suggestions that women are less competent than men at managing security issues.[77] Such stereotyping creates an incomplete and inaccurate picture of what women can contribute, renders important issues invisible and leads to many problems.[78] In contrast, Malathi de Alwis, Julie Mertus, and Tazreena Sajjad suggest that "women should participate in peace processes not because they are innately peaceful or they have been victimized by wars, but because they are themselves political subjects with rights. Women don't need to be better than, or more peaceful than, men to exercise those rights."[79]

In short, using instrumentalist arguments to justify women's inclusion to those in power may come at a high price—one that may even be too high.[80] Thus, rather than making an instrumentalist case here, I follow Enloe's proposition that if policy makers, humanitarian agency staff, members of community organizations, and scholars ignore careful gendered analysis, "we will fail to understand" what we are dealing with and will base "subsequent decisions on flawed expectations."[81]

In the end, relying exclusively on an instrumentalist or operational effectiveness argument may limit prospects for attaining both gender equity and peace and security. It can also clearly hinder implementation of the stated goals of the WPS agenda. To some degree, the false dichotomy of instrumentalist versus rights-based approaches can be a distraction from other possible alternative understandings. As Charlotte Anderholt has argued, including women in formed police units "is both a moral issue and a question of operational effectiveness."[82] Women are not a panacea, but they do have a lot to contribute and deserve fair conditions and recognition. In other words, the presence of women in the broader culture and institutions of peacekeeping is necessary but not sufficient. A one-off addition of a number of women cannot solve the existing gendered problems of pursuing peace and security. At the same time, women deserve the right to participate in decision making around security, become economically empowered, and have access to more diverse and responsive officials providing security and security training.

Overall, the findings of researchers in India and the data gathered in this study challenge the assumption that women in the security sector aspire to change the system or otherwise help women just because they are themselves women. Nonetheless, it is worth noting that FFPU members do work to help women, through both their official duties and their second shift of providing humanitarian and educational services to the community on a volunteer basis. Both their official tasks and their second-shift work have led to important outcomes for women and girls where the FFPU officers are deployed.

LOCAL POLITICAL ECONOMIC OUTCOMES FOR WOMEN IN THE HOST COUNTRY

The political economic approach to women's role in preventing and reducing violence provides an important perspective for reflection and action, concerning not only women in peacekeeping but also local women in host countries. After all, through the "peacekeeping economy," "peacekeepers—as individuals—and peacekeeping—as a complex of institutions, policy and practice—interact with, and inevitably shape, the societies in which they operate."[83] A "peacekeeping economy" then refers to the economic activities that would occur at a lower scale or pay rate, or not occur at all, without the international actors present and the UN peacekeeping mission acting as a central component.[84] This necessarily includes all economic activity, including that of individuals not directly working with or for international organizations.[85]

Research suggests that in the host communities where peacekeeping units are deployed local women are particularly vulnerable. While real job opportunities arise for them as well as for local men, their jobs—typically service jobs—are less well paid, and both local men and local women tend to be less well paid than their international counterparts.[86] Further, local women are more likely to enter potentially exploitative sexual relationships with peace operations personnel.[87] Thus peacekeeping economies and the ways men and women participate in them are most often structured in ways that reflect stereotypical gender roles, where men act as peacekeepers and women may act as underpaid sex workers.[88]

In stark contrast to this are stories from the FFPU's deployment to Liberia, where their presence has been credited with challenging gender stereotypes and encouraging local women to obtain good government jobs in the security sector. Since UNMIL began featuring a highly visible, critical mass of women through the FFPU, many local women have seen such jobs as more possible to obtain and have joined the local police force or served in other security sector roles. This has had broader ramifications in terms of increasing local women's access to resources and decision making in the political and economic realms.

The FFPU's work in communities has also been influential, both for the women joining the police force in Liberia and for women and girls in the communities more broadly. For example, female officers in a UNMIL program aimed at recruiting and training women for careers in the Liberian National Police reported that participating in the program had led to "an increase in the livelihoods for women who have participated . . . and a new inspiration to seek further educational opportunities."[89] These outcomes were directly linked to their mentoring by UN women police, as most of the Liberian women completing the program said it was support from their UN counterparts that kept them in the program.[90]

Notably, this UNMIL program, which was created to serve women lacking the educational requirements for joining the Liberian National Police by offering them a three-month academic program and a three-month police-training program, diverges from the dominant UN approach of favoring instrumentalist over right-based arguments for women's inclusion in the security sector.[91] Its basis was the Liberian National Police's Gender Policy, which includes a 20 percent quota (raised after an original 15 percent quota) for women's participation and "measures to facilitate improved recruitment and retention of women."[92] As focus group discussants have pointed out, the program has seen a steady increase in the number of women participants because of the "multiplier effect" of having earlier graduates of the program in the community show "women that they too, can join LNP."[93] Research has found that local women have been very supportive of such attempts at gender balancing.[94]

Liberians and those working in Liberia have noted many changes since the FFPU arrived. For example, one resident noted that three years into the FFPU's presence, "The number of girls enrolling in school [had] risen dramatically . . . [to a] ratio . . . of girls to boys 70–30. In a nation where few girls are finishing primary school this result is staggering."[95] Moreover, many girls who took community classes with the FFPU "spoke about the personal confidence and esteem they learned from the Indian police-women in their midst."[96]

Overall, it appears that many benefits accrue from the second shift of the FFPU members. Local people, particularly women, in the host country receive needed medical care. Students receive food, learning materials, and lessons in new skills. Young people, especially young women, learn about—and some eventually take up—career opportunities in the security sector. Moreover, the FFPU members themselves can develop a positive feeling of purpose and meaning in their work from these community activities.

However, it is still important to recognize that this is a second shift and something that, if expected of women peacekeepers, should be fairly recognized and expected of men too. After all, if women peacekeepers are expected to role-model ways women can challenge gender norms and be the best women/humans they can be, why shouldn't men working as peacekeepers do the same? This could in fact provide important role modeling for alternative expressions of masculinity following armed conflict, yet because it is not seen as "natural" work for men it is not discussed or expected. What I am suggesting here is that the important work of pursuing gender equity, peace, and security will require efforts around deconstructing gender stereotypes that foster violence and hinder peacebuilding. Women should not shoulder this burden alone, either as peacekeepers or in communities more broadly.

The factors outlined here point to the need for a diverse and nuanced approach to understanding the political economic implications of women's involvement in peacekeeping from various angles. The multiple roles FFPU officers play may be apparent to both their host country and the deploying country and may lead to better opportunities for future career advancement upon their return home, as compared to opportunities for women who were deemed police yet tasked only with cooking and cleaning. Moreover, while women can make crucial contributions in protecting and serving other women as well as children, it is important to avoid pigeonholing their roles so that their careers are seen as only or predominantly relevant in gender-specific or gender-focused contexts.

The presence and practice of the FFPU, then, appears to facilitate economic empowerment for women and girls in a number of ways: (1) upholding the rights of women and girls to both access and participate in security institutions, (2) supporting women's and girls' access to education, and (3) providing decent, comparatively well-paid employment.

The women peacekeepers studied here highlighted meaning, money, and opportunity as key factors in their decision to join the police service and deploy as peacekeepers on a foreign mission. Similar stories and reasons for joining were provided by other research participants—individual female police officers from around the world working in mixed-gender environments in UNMIL, the same mission where the FFPU serves. These questions could be further explored fruitfully in future research, since enhanced recruitment of women will require targeted action, research, and the provision of public information.[97] Indeed, broader understandings of why and how women are recruited to the police service in general and peacekeeping in particular are needed, as this has been given little attention to date. Innovation is also needed. For example, experiments with gender-sensitive budgeting policies, such as "additional monetary incentives for troop-contributing countries to actually include women on missions that could use their assistance," could be advantageous in linking up more strongly political economic approaches and peace and security approaches.[98]

The implications of the FFPU go beyond simply empowering the individual women participating, because peacekeepers and peacekeeping institutions, through the peacekeeping economy, inevitably interact with and influence the societies of the host countries where they are deployed.[99] Through their influence the women peacekeepers of the FFPU and the peacekeeping institutions that sustain them may effect broader social changes that enhance gender equity and security. At the same time, following feminist critiques of militarized citizenship, nuance is needed here to avoid suggesting that work traditionally seen as men's domain, such as policing and peacekeeping, should be valued over other kinds of citizenship or other forms of state service, as this hierarchy marginalizes prospects for women's full citizenship.[100]

The point is not that women *should* take up security sector roles or other male-dominated occupations to achieve greater economic security or recognition of full citizenship. Rather, participation in the security sector and specifically peacekeeping can offer many significant avenues for women's economic empowerment and the broader pursuit of human security. Consequently, states and international organizations *should* make more space for women, including reflecting on ways they may be marginalized from participation or may face extra burdens of "second shift" work even when employed as security sector personnel. As will be explored in the next chapter, this necessarily means critically shifting from neoliberal economic approaches, in which the individual must fit into the system, to approaches that instead focus on changing the system to accommodate a marginalized group—or shifting from thinking about how women can adapt to get a seat at the peacekeeping table, to asking Maha Muna's more challenging question, "Why are there so many men around this table to begin with?"[101]

5 Who's Afraid of the Girls?

FEARS ABOUT FFPUS

*They're either capable or they're not. If not, they shouldn't
deploy. But not only are they capable, they are excellent.
No one ever asked if we should have an all-male unit. Why
should we ask if all-female?*

Mark Kroeker, former civilian police advisor to the UN Police
Division and the UN Department of Peacekeeping Operations

Up until now little progress has occurred around gender mainstreaming in peacekeeping.[1] India's creation of the all-female formed police unit (FFPU) offers new ways to think about gender mainstreaming and women's participation in global security in contrast to typical approaches that rely on women's ability and willingness to fit into male-dominated institutions and male-dominated policing units. In evaluating broader meanings of the FFPU in the global normative environment, it is crucial to explore not only the logics driving this policy innovation but also the logics contesting it. In countering existing global norms around how gender mainstreaming is pursued through the UN, FFPUs challenge policy makers, humanitarian agency staff, and members of community organizations seeking to go beyond official rhetoric to achieve gender equality in practice.

The notion that mixed-gender units are the only and best option for including women remains dominant, despite evidence that women face many barriers to participating in mixed-gender contexts and may have many sound reasons for choosing not to do so. Gender equity has become more recognized as crucial for sustainable peace, marking a significant shift from previous global norms. Yet existing global culture understands gender mainstreaming as women fitting into male-oriented institutions.

UN officials have thus tended to dislike or distrust policy options—like the FFPU—that counter existing gender mainstreaming norms and to distance themselves and the organization from the implementation of such practices, despite their perceived effectiveness and public approval.

Strictly adhering to existing global culture around gender mainstreaming without considering alternatives that might better promote women's rights or enhance effectiveness may limit or stall the inclusion of more women in peacekeeping. It may also obscure aspects of the problem of women's limited inclusion in peace and security processes and ways of understanding whether and how women peacekeepers can contribute where they are deployed. In contrast to mixed-gender formed police units (FPUs), which have received many gendered critiques, FFPUs may provide an alternative or additional option for women wishing to pursue roles as peacekeepers yet not wishing to take on many burdens that women in male-majority units have reportedly faced. Indeed, at present mixed-gender units may well pose significant barriers to increased participation by women that could be addressed to some degree by FFPUs.[2]

To explore these points, this chapter, after defining global culture and current understandings of gender mainstreaming, describes UN officials' views on the FFPU concept. The data gathered suggests that the group's presence raises a number of common gendered fears, expressed by both men and women, around women's roles and capabilities as well as around what constitutes "good" or "real" participation by women. These understandings evidence two different kinds of fears: those based on stereotypical assumptions that women should not engage in peacekeeping and those based on a liberal-informed tendency to be suspicious of gender "segregation" in all forms. The chapter concludes by summarizing the broader implications of the reliance on existing norms around gender mainstreaming in global culture.

THE GLOBAL CULTURE OF GENDER MAINSTREAMING

To understand how the FFPU represents a divergence from norms of "global culture," it is necessary to consider the term itself. Peacekeeping, as an effort undertaken by humans and communicating meaning, is necessarily influenced by cultural considerations.[3] After all, as Sharon Hays points out, culture influences both what we think about and "*how* we think about it."[4] Consequently culture affects peacekeeping in many ways and at many levels.[5] Here I consider the function of "global culture" in UN peacekeeping practice around gender mainstreaming.

According to Roland Paris, the international normative environment—"global culture"—significantly influences the way peacekeeping is understood and carried out. Peacekeeping institutions and their components design and put in place strategies that reflect norms conforming to global culture. At the same time, they reject strategies that diverge from existing norms, even when these might have a greater chance of achieving the goals of peacekeeping.[6] Thus "Global culture limits the range of possible policies that peacekeepers can realistically pursue."[7]

Drawing on the work of James March and Johan Olsen, Paris proposes that the logics of appropriateness (in light of global norms) and effectiveness are not mutually exclusive, and any political action relies on elements of each.[8] In focusing on how the "appropriateness" logic shapes peacekeeping, he argues that looking deeper at how global culture affects peacekeeping can improve our bases for understanding reasons for behavior of those charged with peacekeeping.[9] This may partly be driven by external pressure, as outside actors make efforts to hold the UN to its stated principles and policies.[10] At the same time, international organizations such as the UN also have internal cultural norms that influence how individuals working within the organization understand and interact with the outside world.[11] As a policy maker, Anne Marie Goetz, formerly chief advisor on Peace and Security for UN Women, says, "You cannot risk your project by taking the critical perspective that you could as an academic. . . . It means that there is sometimes too much that can't be said."[12]

The character of peacekeeping is not "determined" by global culture; rather, global norms significantly and repeatedly shape the way peace operations are designed and conducted, though those charged with peacekeeping can also opt to resist existing norms by implementing policies and practices that challenge them.[13] Moreover, as global norms are evolving concurrently with international behavior, shifts in norms can over time lessen concerns about particular policies or practices that are currently seen as normatively unacceptable.[14] Paris suggests that peacekeeping institutions will dismiss out of hand strategies seen as contravening existing global norms without considering their chances of enhancing effectiveness or peacebuilding, as sometimes worries about norm adherence will be prioritized over reflections on operational effectiveness.[15] In analysis of the FFPU, global culture norms relating to gender in peacekeeping are particularly relevant.

While the military, the police, and peacekeeping operations have long been understood as traditionally masculine and occupied predominantly by men, in recent decades the global community through the UN has supported the notion that women ought to have equal access to participation in these areas. Mady Segal suggests that if women are going to participate more in institutions like militaries those institutions must adapt to be more compatible with women, or women must be transformed in ways that make them appear better adapted to serving there.[16] From this perspective, cultural change can lead to structural change, but structural changes can also lead to culture adapting to justify those structural changes.[17] And as structures continue to change, culture may also.[18] Segal claims that when social values relating to gender become more egalitarian, women will join institutions such as the military (and policing or peacekeeping, presumably) in greater numbers.[19] At the same time, Annica Kronsell argues that institutions and subjects are mutually constitutive, so that when institutions historically seen as masculine, such as UN peacekeeping, become more open to "others"—for instance, by rejecting rigid gender segregation—significant potential for changing and developing the institution arises and with it opportunities for altering gender relations.[20]

How does this apply to the current issue of gender mainstreaming in peace and security initiatives? Gaining popularity in the early 1990s, the concept of gender mainstreaming emerged from feminist theory and moved to application in policy;[21] it was purported to shift the focus away from "women's issues," instead asserting the political importance of breaking down traditional roles for men and women and gender-integrating traditionally "masculine" and "feminine" occupations.[22] Emerging as a radical concept driving policy innovation, the controversial goal was to alter existing political and social frameworks that resulted in gendered outcomes.[23] Gender mainstreaming gained support through rapid, global norm diffusion, including UN General Assembly endorsement in 1996 and Resolution 1325 (2000), which asks member states to mainstream gender across all peacekeeping missions.[24] Consequently, "[gender] mainstreaming has become a central component of peacekeeping and peacebuilding operations worldwide."[25] In peacekeeping practice, this has often been understood to mean pursuing gender balance in operations. Gender balancing aims to achieve equal participation by women and men across all activities of a particular institution.[26] The concept has been most particularly adopted in postconflict activities.[27]

In recent years, gender mainstreaming has been understood as the UN's central tool for better including women and has been espoused and taken on by the majority of the biggest, most powerful international agencies.[28] According to the UN Economic and Social Council, gender mainstreaming is "the process of assessing the implications for women and men of any planned action, including legislation, policies or programmes, in all areas and at all levels. It is a strategy for making women's as well as men's concerns and experiences an integral dimension of the design, implementation, monitoring and evaluation of policies and programmes in all political, economic and societal spheres so that women and men benefit equally and inequality is not perpetuated. The ultimate goal is to achieve gender equality."[29]

While initially a radical notion that involved pursuing gender equality through developing policies specifically for women, gender mainstreaming has been defined as requiring programs and institutions to take both men and women into account.[30] But exactly *how* women may be "legitimately" included in areas where they have faced historic marginalization is left ambiguous. In fact, gender mainstreaming has been criticized for being abstract and therefore understood differently within and between governments and nongovernmental organizations.[31] Research has found that many UN staff readily admitted they did not know what gender mainstreaming might include or how they could implement it in their work.[32] Since translating the term can be difficult, stakeholders may come to a wide variety of interpretations of its meaning.[33] Moreover, as the term can be extremely oversimplified or can have threatening connotations in some languages, the process has sometimes been ignored or inaccurately pursued, leading to results that may cause more harm than good.[34] Implementation has differed significantly across countries, as at the national level the norm has been interpreted in ways that greatly vary, at least in part because the norm itself is vague.[35] Consequently, "Implementation ranges from changing existing processes to reaffirming the status quo. The varying interpretations make it difficult to determine precisely what constitutes a breach of the norm."[36]

Given this context, it is unsurprising that contestations of the way gender mainstreaming can be implemented and what constitutes a breach of norms pertaining to gender mainstreaming came up regularly in my own research on the FFPU. In particular, it became clear that many UN staff saw FFPUs as "not the right kind" of gender mainstreaming. In terms of the existing global culture of peacekeeping, the approach of having all-female units was often deemed not appropriate or legitimate, regardless of how it might support the upholding of rights or operational effectiveness.

GENDERED SKEPTICISM AT THE UNITED NATIONS

Putting together and deploying the FFPU required overcoming many hurdles, including the opposition to women's participation in peacekeeping from those not on board with gender mainstreaming generally and opposition to FFPUs specifically as "not the right kind" of gender mainstreaming because of concerns that it introduced "gender segregation." However, notably this latter concern emerged only around all-female units; the same actors failed to express any such concerns about the long-standing presence of all-male units.

In many of the most developed regions in the globe, such as North America, Australia, and Europe, police organizations are clearly gender integrated, even though they sometimes include gender-based violence specializations.[37] Indeed, "Western" or "global North" countries such as these have tended to see gender segregation in policing as an unattractive option whose disadvantages would be greater than its advantages.[38] Likewise, Sarah Hautzinger argues that many of the difficulties that all women's police efforts have faced stem from the same cause—their sex segregation, which can also arguably be seen as their greatest asset.[39]

The interviews cited here highlight that many UN officials' understandings of the FFPU reflect a suspicion of "gender segregation" in all forms (though in practice applied only to all-female spaces or policies), with little discussion of whether or how it may affect theory, policy, or practice positively or negatively. The assumption tends to be simply that having separate women-only units is "not a good thing." Gender mainstreaming in peacekeeping has tended to be understood through a perspective that emphasizes the need for women to adapt to existing institutions and norms in gender-integrated programs that were created primarily with men's needs, abilities, and interests in mind. The introduction of FFPUs represents a contested divergence from such assumptions.

As noted earlier, police advisers from both India and the United States who were active at the UN during the decision-making process and initial deployment of the FFPU had a role in supporting the initiative. However, this buy-in was apparently not transferred to New York–based UN staff that joined the organization later. Indeed, a police adviser who served later stated emphatically that the FFPU was not a UN decision but India's decision: in response to the call for more women, India had offered an all-female force. Moreover, the adviser said, the more recent Bangladeshi FFPU also was a member state initiative rather than a UN initiative. It became clear that while some actors within the UN championed this cause, there were also doubters who did not like the FFPU concept because of ideas about women's roles or because they preferred a liberal feminist model for gender mainstreaming. It appeared that the group's presence incited a number of common gendered fears, both about women's roles and capabilities and about what constituted "good" or "real" participation by women.

FEARS OF WOMEN'S PARTICIPATION IN GENERAL

Attitudinal barriers to women's participation in general were evident at the local level of UN involvement in Liberia, where the FFPU was deployed. At least some UN staff on the ground in Liberia at the time of the first FFPU's deployment were against the deployment, and some even actively tried to block it. Salvador Rodriguez, the FPU coordinator in Liberia at the time, explained that a lot of collaboration went into getting the contingent into place, including dealing with negative statements and obstructions from those who opposed the group's deployment. He noted that he and the deputy police commander, a Norwegian woman, "went to the FPU leadership conference and met . . . the first female FPU commander. She said she was trying to get an FFPU going but was meeting with a lot of resistance."

When asked about the process of deploying the first FFPU, an official who came on board later stated, "There was nothing extraordinary about it except it's an all-female formed police unit." Yet that official still noted, "There was particular care taken due to being female." Presumably this "particular care" was not the female peacekeepers' need for extra care, since they were seasoned security professionals. Rather, the extra care was needed to deal with a vocal minority who opposed the introduction of more women into peacekeeping. As the FPU coordinator stated: "Everyone but a few people thought it was a good idea. Logistics was very difficult, but UNMIL [the UN Mission in Liberia] helped us. [One commander] was at first resistant, but then he saw the benefit, though reluctantly. [Another (female) commander] twisted his arm a bit and got it going. The guys didn't want to take on the females."

Some UN officials, both men and women, specifically challenged the assumption that in peacekeeping men should be the sole actors and decision makers. For example, as noted at the start of this chapter, when the legitimacy of the FFPU was questioned, former UN police adviser Kroeker directly challenged those sexist views. Because questions that assume women are not legitimate actors are nonetheless continuously asked, those organizing the FFPU's deployment from India had to ensure that the FFPU could be deployed in conditions in which they could successfully do their jobs. According to Rodriguez, "Credit goes to the Indian government because before moving or deciding to send them [the Indian general] wanted to send officers to make sure they weren't sending them into an abyss. And he came out as a guest of [the UN Mission in Liberia], and he and Seema [Dhundia, FFPU commander] came to check it out themselves for a week and a half to tour around Liberia and see where camps and plans would be and what training."

While those who resented or rejected women's participation in peacekeeping made the job of implementing the FFPU more difficult, in the end they were merely another obstacle to overcome.

FEARS ABOUT ALL-WOMEN'S UNITS

Those pushing for the FFPU's introduction also met with challenges from actors at the UN who believed that single-gender units, at least in the case of women, could not be legitimate. As Kroeker recounted, when the idea of the FFPU first came up, people asked, "Do they have the right equipment, qualifications, and is the mission willing to have them? . . . The questions started coming: Are you sure an all-woman unit is really appropriate?"

Such questions are very commonly asked about women-only units making incursions into areas that have been historically unquestioned for being all-male spaces. For example, when an all-women contingent was created in the Civilian Protection Component of the Mindanao People's Caucus in the Philippines' Mindanao conflict region, the organization's secretary-general Mary Ann Arnado reported being asked almost exactly the same questions: "Are these women trained? Can they possibly do it? Will they be effective? Can they make a difference?"[40]

Arnado's response challenged the veiled sexism and inherent instrumentalism such questions rely on, and implicitly voiced a more rights-based approach: "Why is it that women should bear the burden of proof of showing that they could make a difference while the men have long been making a total mess of our security situation? Again, the naughty answer can be, "Well we don't even have to make a difference. Like you, we have the right to be here. Period."[41] Part of what is interesting about this is the notion that this would be a "naughty" answer, as opposed to a straightforward response to an unfairly loaded question that undermines women's authority and capacity to participate in peacekeeping. In the UN as in Mindanao, the people who questioned the introduction of FFPUs—solely on the basis of gender—whether all-female units could be "effective" or "fair"—were not asking those same questions of the previous all-male units.

At the global level, this may be related to the allegation of a "bias against gender equality within the United Nations system, a function of the myriad of identities and associated 'baggage' that staff personnel bring to their jobs, as well as flaws in the personnel and human resources management structures."[42] Angela Raven-Roberts notes that, despite resolutions on gender balance, little change has occurred in several key UN bodies, including the Department of Peacekeeping Operations.[43] Moreover, when the UN has implemented "affirmative actions"—such as special efforts to recruit more women, requirements for training in gender sensitivity, and the appointment of "gender focal points," or staff focused on supporting the implementation of gender mainstreaming— the response has been "a great deal of bitterness in some male staff who see their years of accumulated experience being washed away by a tide of new 'token' women appointees."[44]

In the Department of Peacekeeping Operations in particular, a number of actors have expressed concerns that "using quotas for women tends to generate a perception that women are there because of the quota rather than as a result of their needed skills and competencies."[45] Again this is interesting in that it reifies the assumption that somehow all men in previously all-male units got there solely because they possessed the needed skills and competencies, rather than, for example, possessing the body type and gender performance most strongly associated with a "natural" disposition to provide security or peacekeeping, or their connections to male decision makers in police, military, or other security sector roles. Women, when appearing in roles *as* women, were often subject to scrutiny and suspicion of their perceived inadequacies, while men's possibly unearned privilege as sole actors in peacekeeping remained unexamined.

In this environment, UN staff, especially those who started working for the UN in New York after the initial deployment, did not see the introduction of the first FFPU or those that followed as meeting UN needs or requests or even really fitting UN intentions. Indeed, a later police adviser shared this hesitant position, stating, "We were on one hand pleased, but it really wasn't what we were on about with gender mainstreaming. We'd rather see a mixed-gender contingent like the Nigerians." Those who worked with mixed-gender contingents in Liberia reported that women who deployed in male-majority units as police officers were often tasked mostly with jobs like cooking and cleaning on arrival, leaving little chance that they would gain significant police experience while deployed, yet those women reportedly appeared as more legitimate, appropriate peacekeeping actors in the UN context.

Furthermore, two current UN staff members emphasized as a key point that the FFPU had to be "the same quality" as their male colleagues. Interestingly, when a new men's unit is deployed in these roles there does not appear to be an inherent concern that this particular group of men will not be equal to the previous group. The question seems to arise only because the contingent in question is entirely staffed by women. A former high-ranking UN official who served in Liberia also noted that, although she saw how professional and successful the group was, she still,

> heard the FFPU of India was not one of the best we have professionally. People say it's just because they're women and not on par, and I think it's dangerous. I remember once in Nigeria . . . they entertained the idea of an FFPU, but I said, "You can have mixed units, so why don't you do that?" That's why I underline that they [the Indian FFPU] are very professional. I don't want them to be a token of gender parity. Then I think it's dangerous that if you signal to be a female in the national police force you can succeed by being less qualified. Then it's a short-term success rather than a sustainable one.

Again this indicates a problem where women, without a substantiated basis but solely because of their gender, are often assumed to be tokens, less qualified, and less professional. Yet these assumptions do not tend to be made about male peacekeepers solely on the basis of their gender.

Although some officials recognized the FFPU's positive contributions, many were uncomfortable with or outright objected to their being an all-female unit. Nonetheless, even a current staffer who adamantly disagreed with the introduction of an all-female unit, stating a preference for gender "integration" and saying that FPUs were "a lesser form of policing," did admit, after visiting them, that "They were impressive." Moreover, one former high-ranking UN official who was in Liberia with the FFPU stated "It was extremely important that they were women and protected their gender, but it wouldn't have worked if they weren't professional. If not the best, they were one of the best professionally. They happened to be women, and it demonstrated the importance of women in the security."

Still, as mentioned earlier, this official too was hesitant about extending the policy of introducing FFPUs more broadly, saying, "I think it's fine, but I want to underline that the goal is not to have a lot of FFPUs. It's to showcase women in policing to then get gender parity in national forces. I think it would be very well justified if we have these challenges about deploying women and men side by side, fine, but I'm nervous that our goal is to make the national police force functional, and I cannot see that would be through separate men and women's units. It should work as an integrated force."

For officials like this one, who supported women's participation in the security sector, such hesitancy often appeared to come from a position of seeking to avoid the chance for detractors to make unfounded accusations that women were unqualified tokens. That is, the hesitancy was not based on any concern that a peacekeeping unit staffed by women would be unable to meet the demands of their job, but rather on how the unit might fit within broader aims of the UN and perceptions about what the UN supported. In other words, challenges could emerge between integrating the UN's day-to-day operational goals with its long-term aspirational goals.

BROADER IMPLICATIONS OF THE FEARS RAISED BY FFPUS

These explorations confirm some significant theoretical observations that have been made in the existing literature. For one, objections to the FFPU on the grounds of their being women bring to mind Cynthia Enloe's discussion of the anxiety created around femininity when women are mobilized in wartime situations and concern grows about whether such participation will lead to their losing "their supposedly essential feminine qualities: domesticity, sexual reserve, emotional sensitivity, and maternalism."[46] At the same time, those questioning the women's capacity solely on the basis of their being women reconfirm that often men remain "the unmarked, default category—the generic *human* against which others are compared and potentially deviate."[47] In other words, legitimate participation for women is defined as participating "like men" in mostly-male units. The UN's tendency to rely on norms of global culture around implementing gender mainstreaming has broader implications on a global scale, where gender norms regularly impede women's potential to participate in peacekeeping, as well as their ability to be heard in peace processes, both formally and informally.

As shown in this case, those seeking to implement and expand this innovative policy have encountered obstacles. Some obstacles have been individual, as when initially certain UN staff members on the ground in Liberia did not want women peacekeepers coming in to participate. Other obstacles have been structural, as when UN policy and policy makers in New York showed a preference for a normative framework, tying equal participation to gender "integration" in peacekeeping. Both of these attitudes to FFPUs can thwart the goal of increasing women's participation in peacekeeping, a goal the United Nations Security Council has explicitly linked with achieving and sustaining peace.

The dominant UN view of gender mainstreaming as synonymous with gender integration has meant involving women as a small minority in a male-led group, with possible material, cultural, and practical challenges around gendered issues like accommodation and job roles. Relying on such a narrow range of options may obscure important differences that warrant further examination in constructing more nuanced approaches. As Sally Engle Merry argues, gendered identities are located within regionally specific and historically created ethnic and class structures; thus men and women hold "historically produced subject positions, shaped by larger institutional structures and adopted or discarded only within the constraints of wealth, color, and class."[48] These differing identities, locations, and subject positions can lead to differences in focus of movements combating violence against women. Uma Narayan, in her study looking at discussions around "dowry deaths" in India and domestic violence in the United States, argues that such "asymmetries in focus" relate to the different ways issues of violence against women come up within, and have been addressed by, women's movements in different locations.[49]

As Mark Goodale and Sally Engle Merry explain, today's international and transnational actors aiming to end violence against women may see this as a fairly straightforward goal, yet "the emergence of different means through which these goals are met has created a transnational normative pluralism whose full effects and meanings are still unclear."[50] Indeed, factors influencing feasibility of approaches to addressing violence against women can vary greatly between different contexts.[51] For example, "battered women's shelters" have been seen as successful short-term interventions in the West, but some argue their utility may be limited to particular contexts. These authors suggest that the usefulness of these shelters is dependent on the presence of a welfare system providing things like free schooling for children and subsidized housing, an employment scenario that differs greatly from India's, a low level of stigma against women moving around or living on their own, and the presence of certain employment opportunities that would not be considered appropriate for Indian middle-class women.[52]

In contrast, women in India who separate from their husbands or live "on their own" are far more stigmatized.[53]

Narayan similarly points out that feminist agendas are, and need to be, shaped by different national contexts and the varying conditions women experience within them. This is because issues affecting women are themselves "'shaped' within different national contexts" and because a lack of awareness of these contexts can "affect the project of 'cross-cultural understanding.'"[54] In particular, she suggests that the West and Western feminists, who focus on the "Indianness" of issues such as dowry murders, often poorly understand issues around violence against women in the Third World because they position them as things "that happen elsewhere," focusing on their most extreme and exotic manifestations, and as "unlike 'things that happen here,'" even though, for instance, the rates of dowry murders in India and of spousal killings of women in the United States are similar.[55] Narayan suggests that racism or ethnocentrism alone cannot account for the "distortions" that emerge when issues from the Third World are taken up in Western national contexts.[56] She suggests that "multiple mediations" take place between (1) the ways such issues are shaped in Western contexts, (2) the "life" the issues may have in their home arenas, where the local public have the diverse contextual information needed to see the issues "in perspective," and (3) the decontextualizing and recontextualizing processes that occur as the issues cross national borders.[57] In light of her points, understanding the FFPU and its potential necessarily involves paying attention to both the Indian context from which it has emerged and the culture of the international organization through which it operates—the UN.

The FFPU's challenge to existing norms around gender mainstreaming in peacekeeping may have important effects. By gaining legitimacy through their clearly strong performance, the FFPU may significantly disrupt norms that limit women's involvement in general or restrict their involvement to acting as a small minority in male-majority contingents. As Kroeker explains, "It's put the idea of gender mainstreaming to the test to say, 'We either believe this or we don't.'"

The FFPU could also be seen as a temporary special measure. From this perspective, more FFPUs could be developed alongside existing efforts at increasing gender integration in peacekeeping units. As Charlotte

Anderholt suggests, gaining better representation of women in peace-keeping will require

- promoting practices and policies that address the material and procedural barriers that limit women's likelihood to apply to police units or finish their police training
- collecting evidence to clarify why women do not apply for more police jobs
- countering the male-dominated culture of police agencies within member states
- developing procedures and policies that address barriers to women's deciding to deploy in FPU missions, including respecting and supporting women in the family responsibilities that they carry, typically in contrast to their male counterparts.[58]

Such changes will not happen easily or quickly, but they are necessary. Meanwhile, participation in FFPUs may offer the women who participate in them significant leadership opportunities and relevant security experience that may be used both in later FFPUs and in mixed-gender contingents.

Efforts to create and deploy the FFPU evoked a number of common gendered fears, including fears both of women's participation in security in general and of women's participation specifically in all-female units. The latter set of concerns relate to a global culture of gender mainstreaming in peace-keeping that typically views women's involvement as "legitimate" or "appropriate" only when it comes in the form of participating as a small minority in male-majority units. Sticking to such a limited ideology obscures aspects of the problem of women's limited inclusion in peace processes and ways of understanding whether and how women peacekeepers can contribute to enhancing peace and security where they are deployed.

Attempts to include more women in peacekeeping may be limited or stalled by strict adherence to existing global culture around gender main-streaming and a refusal to critically engage with alternatives that may foster greater traction for achieving gender equity, peace and security. Raising the numbers of women peacekeepers and the impacts of those already deployed requires efforts from both men and women within the UN and beyond, including a willingness to challenge existing gender norms. The case of the

FFPUs—in highlighting an innovative approach to gender mainstreaming in peacekeeping—also tells us important stories about norms. Specifically, it highlights how norms, which are seen here as dynamic and evolving over time, can be shaped by and can shape notions of legitimacy. At the same time, what is seen as legitimate—or appropriate—can be contested and can evolve over time. Looking at legitimacy in this way is important for better understanding the perceptions and intentions of various actors who have a role in shaping the norms.[59]

FFPUs represent an alternative approach to women's inclusion in peacekeeping that gives serious attention to women's needs and motivations. It does so by pursuing gender mainstreaming through structural change to incorporate women as peacekeepers who can access women's spaces, rather than waiting for individual women to decide that the existing male-dominated system is for them. While this approach is not perfect and does not perfectly meet the UN's ultimate goal of having women and men work together side by side to achieve peace and security, it is a timely measure that pragmatically seeks to pursue long-term goals while working with available options in the short term. In doing so, FFPUs may enhance security for women and men here and now.

6 Increasing Women's Participation in Peace and Security

As for me, when we're talking about equality, it should be real equality. I mean, if you can make some quotas, even if it could be 50/50 but not whol[ly a] women's unit . . . or a men's unit. It would be good to have half/half. (Ukraine)

I'd prefer to see more inclusion [of] police officers than formed police units. I think the formed police unit, you've even got to look at the culture of the countries that they come from—and it's like safety in numbers, sending the women over together. . . We've had very few, if any, Indian IPOs [Individual Police Officers] here that are females . . . I think that I'd rather see more [of those] actually than [them] coming as a safe pack. (UK)

As long as they're well trained, I have no objection as to who comes, male or female. If an FFPU [all-female formed police unit] is needed, that's fine. I like someone who knows how to handle a weapon, that's what they are responsible for. (USA)

Female peacekeeping officers serving in mixed-gender environments in Liberia, when asked what they think of the concept of FFPUs

Scholars and policy makers have posited numerous benefits of including women as peacekeepers. Researchers have suggested that the presence of female police has calmed dangerous situations, that female mission staff lead to more "civilized" behavior among the mission staff overall with far fewer criticisms of personal and professional behavior than male staff receive, and

that their inclusion results in more effective missions, which are seen as having added legitimacy.[1] For example, some have argued that the presence of
women means fewer cases of HIV, brothels near peacekeeping bases, and
children abandoned by male peacekeepers after the mission. Moreover,
studies of women peacekeepers compared to their male colleagues show that
women "have significantly lower rates of complaints of misconduct,"
"improper use of force," and "inappropriate use of weapons."[2] In contrast,
there are many high-profile reports of male peacekeepers facing accusations
of sexually abusing or assaulting those they are meant to serve.[3] Plus,
research has found that women peacekeepers "are less authoritarian in interactions with citizens and lower-ranking officers. In addition, women officers
respond more effectively to violence committed against women and are
more likely to respond to domestic abuse claims. Most importantly women
officers are seen as being able to diffuse [*sic*] potentially violent situations
without the use of force more effectively than male counterparts."[4]

In short, many have suggested that women are needed in peacekeeping
at least in part because they can be expected to behave better than their
male counterparts or to influence their male colleagues to behave better.
Indeed, there is evidence that "the presence of women peacekeepers can
and does foster a change in male behavior when women are deployed in
PKOs [peacekeeping operations]."[5] Furthermore, the UN has enumerated
several other benefits from having a strong presence of women peacekeepers, including the creation of safer spaces for women and girls who have
survived sexual violence, increased participation of women in national
police forces, enhanced capacity for calming crowds in riots, and increased
reporting of sexual violence.[6] Sally Engle Merry suggests that when
feminist movements challenge the notion that gendered violence is inevi-
table and inescapable its victims can become more willing to take legal
recourse and justice institutions can become more willing to respect complainants and seriously consider their reports.[7]

Female peacekeepers have thus been cited as especially important in
areas where sexual violence has been a feature of conflict and where there
are cultural prohibitions on women's discussing sexual matters with men.
Several UN agencies have testified that women staff are needed across a
range of the UN's activities and note that this is especially pertinent in
host mission sites where girls and women are unable to interact with

males who are not family members.[8] For example, the UN Food Programme reported that victims often "prefer talking to a woman representing the international community than to fellow refugees about the violence they had suffered."[9] Likewise, Vlachova and Biason state that a lack of female police officers is a barrier to achieving justice, and others have argued that "local women are more likely to report crimes to women police."[10] In fact, researchers have found that reports of sexual assault go up with the number of women in the police force.[11]

Women affected by sexual violence, therefore, continue to face barriers to justice that are related to a lack of female personnel in peace operations. This may be mitigated to some extent where women are deployed as police peacekeepers. A UN police gender adviser in Liberia says, "The presence of female police officers in Liberia ha[s] helped a lot in the reporting of sexual and gender-based violence cases. It is not very easy for a woman to discuss sexual violence issues with a male officer," but they "feel free to bring out their cases" when there are women police available.[12]

Given all these stated benefits, it is no surprise that the UN has cited a need for more women in peacekeeping.[13] Resolution 1820 specifically called for "including wherever possible the deployment of a higher percentage of women peacekeepers or police," and several experts have called for greater numbers of women in policing, the military, cease-fire monitoring, and other security forces.[14] Indeed, getting more women involved in the security sector can create exponentially more involvement, since when women come into contact with other women working in the security sector they are more likely to join the security sector themselves.[15] Finally, some evidence also suggests that gender-balanced groups are more likely to take gender into account and that women's inclusion in decision making results in better policy outcomes for women.[16]

OBSTACLES TO RECRUITING MORE WOMEN IN PEACEKEEPING

Despite the increased attention to gender equity in peace and security and extensive discussions of the perceived benefits that may come from women's participation in peacekeeping, limited headway has been made so far

in terms of increasing it. In 2012, at a regional dialogue in Monrovia enti-
tled "Enhancing Women's Leadership in Peace and Security in West
Africa," the UN Women representative in Liberia, Elizabeth Lwanga, con-
cluded that reform efforts up until now have had little impact: "The
instruments provided by the United Nations such as Resolution 1325
should have led to a better situation on women's leadership in peace processes and peacebuilding."[17] Dialogue participants recommended addressing these issues through extended recruitment of women and strength-
ened support for their roles in the security sector.[18]

By the UN's own report on ten years of impact, attempts to implement
Resolution 1325 in peacekeeping have met with mixed results.[19] While
more states are in principle signing on to the Women, Peace and Security
agenda, creating national action plans for implementing Resolution 1325,
creating support organizations for women officers, increasing women's
security sector participation in administrative and professional roles, supporting women's participation in electoral processes, and creating policies
supporting gender mainstreaming, others aims have seen more modest
outcomes, including protecting women from sexual violence in conflict,
gaining commitment from senior leadership on the WPS agenda, and
increasing the numbers of women peacekeepers.[20] Although many countries have created recruitment policies that aim to be gender sensitive,
very few countries have seen a significant increase of women's propor-
tional participation in national security institutions.[21] Moreover, where
more women have been recruited in police and military roles in peace
support operations, the complex gender implications are not always necessarily positive.[22]

These limited outcomes reflect the many challenges and barriers to
women's participation in peacekeeping:

(1) Nationally, women are less likely to join the security sector to begin
     with.

(2) Internationally, women are less likely to become part of a
     peacekeeping contingent even if they are part of the national police
     service.

(3) In the United Nations, "blue tape" can create structural barriers that
     disproportionately discriminate against women candidates.

(4) In actual peacekeeping deployment, women often face added
challenges and expectations relative to their male counterparts.

These types of barriers are not always distinct, as they can often be related.
For example, women may be less likely to take on a peacekeeping assign-
ment because they are aware of the extra challenges they will face due to
gendered expectations.

THE NATIONAL CONTEXT

There are many obstacles to women's participation in security institutions
at the national level. Charlotte Anderholt classes such obstacles into two
categories: direct discrimination and systemic barriers.[23] The former relates
to the male-dominated culture of police units, while the latter relate to
recruitment and hiring practices that keep many women from applying for
jobs in policing because of the added domestic burdens that women are far
more likely than men to carry. For example, hours are often inflexible and
part-time opportunities may be nonexistent. Moreover, required universal
physical fitness tests are often cited as a barrier to recruiting women. Such
tests are often set using a male baseline, which reduces both the number of
women applying (for fear of failing the test) and the number eligible to be
hired. Such practices persist despite much criticism and questioning of the
scientific evidence that these kinds of standards are necessary to do the
job.[24] Moreover, gender stereotypes of women as physically and emotionally weak have constituted barriers to their participation in peacekeeping.[25]
The UN's own research reports have noted such challenges to women serving in peacekeeping, saying, "The culture of most national security institutions remains unfriendly to women; discrimination and sexual harassment
of female officers are widespread."[26]

Such experiences are also well documented in the wider literature. For
example, in 2008, a female Los Angeles Police Department officer won a
sexual harassment lawsuit against the department, which was found to
have allowed an environment in which her male colleagues "excluded her
from training opportunities," made inappropriate comments, and exposed
their genitalia.[27] As Emma Birikorang found in her research on Liberian

efforts at security sector reform, even programs that have sought to streamline women's paths to careers in national policing have faced difficulties in recruiting women.[28] A UN report on a program designed to recruit women officers there noted that the main reasons for dropping out of the program were "family and social pressures; pregnancy or health issues; financial or transportation limitations."[29] As Sarah Hautzinger points out, women officers may also be held to lofty expectations that lead to their own and the public's disillusionment when these cannot be met.[30] Thus efforts that seek to include more women in the security sector need to attend to motivation and incentives for women to pursue careers in peacekeeping as well as barriers to their involvement.

BARRIERS TO INTERNATIONAL DEPLOYMENT

Even where women have been recruited to participate in national police forces, barriers exist to their deployment in international peacekeeping. Indeed, Anita Schjølset's recent research in Norway has shown that even where a higher percentage of women have been recruited to the military at the national level, success at reducing the gap in participation in international missions has not been achieved.[31] Therefore, she argues that alternative strategies ought to be pursued for targeting women for international military deployments. Statistics also show that US women are underrepresented in UN peacekeeping compared to their proportion of the national armed forces in the United States.[32] Given that policing most often takes place in community contexts, women recruited in domestic police programs may have different motivations that make them even more unlikely to pursue international deployments. Thus attention must be given to identifying and implementing incentives that can motivate and support women to pursue career paths in international peace operations. As former UN Department of Peacekeeping Operations (DPKO) police adviser Kiran Bedi explained, "We get women police officers in peacekeeping only if the member-states forward their names. And usually they do not, even where they have good numbers, the reasons being their own country's needs, women being low on priority compared with men and. . . general indifference. Many countries still have mere symbolic presence of women in police work. Hence, they themselves are in need of correction. But we from the UN are pursuing forcefully the compelling need to increase the presence of qualified women candidates."[33]

Even when women manage to surmount the obstacles to joining their national forces, they may still face discrimination when they want to take on roles in international peacekeeping missions to which their country contributes. For example, one Ukrainian woman working as an individual police officer for the UN Mission in Liberia explained:

> In our country . . . I mean it is common to meet a woman police officer, approximately 20 percent, something like that. But . . . they didn't want to give me this position, not the OIC [officer in command], the chief, only because of my age. I'm thirty, and my boss, he is a man. And in our country, for example, when a woman [gives birth to a] child she has the right to go . . . to maternity leave [for] three years. . . . For us it is very good. But for your promotion, of course, nobody wants to give you a good position because you will leave your job for three years, so it's not possible. And then they're happy that I had such an opportunity to apply for an international position . . . For me I am a bit proud, we have twenty participants from Ukraine in Liberia and two women among them.

In short, it is clear that women may face a variety of context-specific barriers to deploying to international peacekeeping missions even where they already have experience as police in their national services.

One survey of the Royal Canadian Mounted Police, which "has been highly proactive in trying to implement the goals of resolution 1325," found that 69 percent of female officers felt women failed to apply to international peacekeeping missions "because agencies did not proactively recruit women."[34] And even when they are invited to join international policing missions and have a strong interest in doing so, women officers often decline to take up such postings, primarily because of a lack of support for their domestic responsibilities.[35] Rather than moving toward greater flexibility for officers with family responsibilities, one could argue that recent changes pose further barriers. For example, "The [UN] Police Division now requests contributing countries to extend the tour of duty of FPU [formed police unit] personnel from six months to one year."[36] Such policies may further reify the notion that national police services should send only those who are able to spend increasingly long periods away from home. This may well deter them from recruiting women with family responsibilities and may lead those women already in the force to turn down peacekeeping deployments.

"BLUE TAPE" AT THE UNITED NATIONS

Despite existing national and international efforts to support more frequent deployment of women in international peacekeeping operations, there still exists significant "blue tape"—UN policies and practices that may hinder such efforts directly or indirectly. To begin with, traditionally the UN devotes little attention and few resources "to outreach and communication with organizations that can access qualified female candidates, or to marketing these positions in a way that will attract the best talent."[37] Moreover, the barriers the UN sets for participation in peacekeeping may also disproportionately affect women.

Currently, to participate in peacekeeping operations, one must have five years' experience in the force of one's home country, be part of a country supplying police, and be given permission or be chosen by the government to participate in peacekeeping as a police officer. These requirements mean the barriers to women's participation are high. First of all, if a woman, even one who is already a police officer, is interested in working in peacekeeping but lives in a country that does not regularly recruit and deploy police for peacekeeping or offer fair conditions for women's involvement, her access is obstructed. The required number of years of experience may also constitute an unnecessary barrier. For example, having many years of experience in a national police force does not necessarily correlate with ability to adequately address crimes of sexual and gender-based violence in international conflict. After all, as previously noted, most security specialists have little or no training in handling sexual and gender-based violence complaints, one of the major areas women peacekeepers have been expected to address on the basis of stereotypes about their "natural" ability in this area.

Given that women's lives often include interrupted working patterns, the requirement of mid- to senior levels of experience in a national police force before one can even be considered for international operations may be an unnecessary impediment to recruitment of women. The requirements preclude participation by younger women, yet these are the women who may have more flexibility to work abroad, as they may not yet have as many family commitments that require their presence. Women who meet the five-year requirement, in contrast, may be at a life stage that includes family commitments that make them less likely to serve internationally.[38] The recent extension to length of deployments previously mentioned heightens this difficulty. Although the UN Police Division says that implementing less frequent rotations allows them to "to select more qualified FPU candidates, improves the level of professionalism of FPU personnel and directly increases operational capabilities by raising the level of experience among personnel in the field," they do not consider how this might indirectly discriminate against potential female recruits. Interestingly, in discussions of this topic the DPKO did note that longer deployments would necessitate "greater welfare considerations," but they emphasized only "the need to deploy adequate sports and recreation equipment to boost the morale of FPU personnel,"[39] which appears inadequate to address the welfare concerns of women with family responsibilities who might like to serve. This is particularly salient given that reports have highlighted that the vast majority of women serving in the FFPU are mothers. In short, recruitment and deployment strategies that take the independent male figure with no family responsibilities as the starting point seem unlikely to see much advancement in terms of recruiting more women to the field.

Finally, one practical limitation has been that the existing infrastructure caters to single-sex units, which have historically been male. As former UN DPKO police adviser Mark Kroeker explained, "FPUs live together tightly in camps and dorms, so it's easier to be single gender when living in tents together. The time is coming when, with proper accommodation, like in military operations, we send women all the time."

Although FPUs usually rely on the deploying country to supply accommodation, practical issues associated with accommodation may be rectified soon through international efforts. Work is under way at the UN Logistics Base in Brindisi, Italy, to produce architectural plans that will be used for developing modular policing infrastructure. According to the DPKO, "The standardized modular structures are being designed to be easily, quickly and inexpensively deployed. The goal of the project is to make it possible for UN Police and national counterparts in countries where the UN is deployed to be able to construct or obtain standard modules that can be used and linked to create standardized police stations, offices, accommodations, training facilities, police cells, mobile police centres, armouries, command and control centres and police academies."[40]

BARRIERS TO FULL PARTICIPATION AS PEACEKEEPERS

Even once women are deployed in international peacekeeping, they face barriers to full participation. When, as is usually the case, they are deployed as part of male-majority units, they may encounter tension with their male colleagues, an absence of social support, and a general lack of gender-sensitive approaches.[41] They may have the double burden of trying to meet high expectations while themselves facing dangers of sexual harrassment and exploitation from both local forces and their own colleagues, and even being expected to mediate conflicts between men in their own contingent.[42]

Research on female Norwegian peacekeepers suggests the need to temper heightened expectations of special contributions women can make in peacekeeping, as they reported that local people "react[ed] to their uniform 'not [their] sex.'"[43] Indeed, research has suggested that women in the masculine military setting of peacekeeping operations tend to accept and internalize the "boys will be boys" attitude as shared by and applied to their male colleagues.[44] Some research has found female peacekeepers unwilling to report sexual abuse and exploitation offenses committed by their male colleagues against locals.[45] When action is not taken in such cases, it can erode the trust of local women, making them unwilling to report offenses to peacekeepers.

Although women peacekeepers have been assumed to be "naturally" inclined to help address women's issues, the hypermasculine environment often found in male-majority units may mean that only women who are the least interested in working with or supporting other women seek to join such units. Liora Sion, for example, noted that the women in the mixed-gender units she studied "preferred men's presence to women's," with one explaining, "I get along well with the guys. . . . I wouldn't like to serve with a platoon full of women, I don't think I would be able to get along with them, I'm used to working with men."[46] Thus women who join such male-dominated groups must be willing to act as "one of the boys," downplaying any aspects of their gender or sexuality so that it cannot be held against them in an environment that does not value femininity.[47] At the same time, many communicated ambivalence about femininity or sought to avoid it by avoiding interacting with other women and mocking those who were seen as stereotypically female.[48] Such attitudes may be developed or reinforced in contexts where ideas and actors associated with femininity are delegitimized.

This may relate to findings from research on women's participation as political representatives in democracies. Although female politicians report more liberal attitudes around topics seen as "women's issues," there are few differences in the policy proposals they make compared to male colleagues. This situation of not translating their ideas into policy has been explained as caused by the general lack of acceptance of women in the institution, so that the women there are unwilling to gamble their own standing to take on issues their male colleagues do not see as legitimate.

Some challenges faced by women peacekeepers appear to be particular to their participation in male-majority units. As their gendered status coincides with the minority position in this context, women may face challenges of tokenism.[49] They also tend to hold traditionally feminine roles, like medical-related positions or administrative jobs.[50] The FPU coordinator in Liberia at the time of the first FFPU deployment recalled the FFPU commander stating that integration of men and women in peacekeeping units tended to create some problems. For example, he said, the Nigerian peacekeeping force at the time was 80 percent male and 20 percent female, but the women cooked, cleaned, and did administrative work, not policing. For this reason, UN reports have described the inclusion of female peacekeepers in mixed-gender Nigerian and Ghanaian Battalions as "a *potential* best practice, not as a best practice. The reason is that these peacekeepers hold supportive as opposed to direct impact roles."[51]

Research suggests that women's restriction to gender-stereotypical roles in peacekeeping is often the result, not of their own preferences or choices, but of stereotypes applied to them by their male colleagues and the institutions they serve. For example, according to Vandra Harris and Andrew Goldsmith's study on Australian policewomen serving in police peacekeeping roles in East Timor, women reported facing "gender-based exclusion within the UN police force, including exclusion of women from front-line policing in spite of their relevant experience."[52] And a UN policy dialogue on enhancing gender balance in peacekeeping reported concerns about women peacekeepers' restriction to "tasks designated as 'women's issues,' such as working on sexual violence or family support issues," and urged instead that they be "assigned to work on a whole range of peace-building functions."[53]

But when women step outside such restrictions and take on roles that are male dominated, including policing, research shows they have a significant likelihood of being harassed, and if they fail to follow gender stereotypes the harassment levels tend to increase.[54] According to one unpublished United Nations report, for example, female police officers in Afghanistan reported "pervasive sexual violence and harassment by their male colleagues."[55] Similarly, Harris and Goldsmith's study of Australian women peacekeepers in East Timor found that the women's most commonly reported difficulties stemmed from the hostility and sexist behavior of their male colleagues.[56] These challenges often arise when women are isolated as tokens in a hypermasculine space.[57]

PROSPECTS AND CHALLENGES FOR WOMEN'S PARTICIPATION IN PEACEKEEPING THROUGH FFPUS

Given the problems that women peacekeepers encounter in male-majority units, the introduction of all-female units might assuage some of these concerns. Offering the option of participating in an all-female contingent with a few male support staff does not solve these problems on a broader level, but it does ensure that in these cases the women are able to draw on their relevant experience and take on key roles in ensuring peace and security. These roles may be apparent to both their host country and the deploying country and may give women better opportunities for future career advancement upon their return home than the prospects of women in male-majority units who were deemed police but tasked only with cooking and cleaning.

Research has found that international forces modeling gender equality are more likely to lead to increases in political participation among local women and decreases in domestic violence in the host society.[58] Though benefits may also accrue from simply having more women present, even in a sex-segregated unit, deploying women-only units may benefit both the women involved as police and the local communities. Mangai Natarajan, in her extensive research on the Indian domestic policing experience, found that all-women units operating domestically within India's national police service built the confidence of women police, enhanced their professionalism, and provided effective and efficient policing.[59]

The FFPU in Liberia has contributed to the local population not only by keeping the peace but by serving as role models for women and children and volunteering for numerous community tasks outside their main duties as peacekeepers—activities that apparently are not expected from male peacekeepers. They have been noted for "encouraging literacy among women" and "providing skills training to youths, especially girls"—for example, the summer camp for girls that teaches first aid and self-defense.[60] As noted earlier, the FFPU also offers clean drinking water and free medical care in accessible areas near schools and hospitals.[61] This has been linked with better overall security, as the UN Mission in Liberia has suggested that reducing competition for scarce resources in this way has helped instill calm and reduce petty crimes driven by poverty.[62]

Finally, the FFPU has increased interest among Liberian women about taking on security sector roles. Reports from outside the UN indicate a significant increase in the number of women recruited into the Liberian National Police since the group's introduction.[63] Indeed, US ambassador Shirin Tahir-Kheli stated that "the effect on Liberian women was reported to be significant and almost immediate: the number of women applying to join the LNP [Liberian National Police] tripled from approximately 120 to 350 in the two months after the arrival of the first FPU."[64] This may be partly because the presence of the FFPU increases awareness that women can take on such roles, and partly because FFPU officers also participate in activities such as visiting and speaking at high schools and universities and at career fairs.[65]

Moreover, the indirect impacts of the Indian FFPU in Liberia have been felt much further afield. For example, the Indian FFPU reportedly "inspired the launch of a women's corps in the peacekeeping contingent of the Civil Protection Component (CPC) of the Malaysia-led International Monitoring Team (IMT) in Mindanao, Philippines."[66] It also inspired Nigeria and Bangladesh to create their own all-female units and encouraged other countries like Ghana and Rwanda to increase their contributions of female troops in UN missions.[67] This may be related to the claim that imposing Western gender "integration" models on policing is not always effective in different contexts, which may require more culturally sensitive approaches.[68] At the same time, given that after the FFPU's introduction, Liberia reached a significantly higher percentage of women police than the USA, one could argue that existing approaches to gender integration in policing do not necessarily work so well even in the contexts that have typically proposed and supported them. In any case, the findings presented here regarding the FFPU confirm and add to Karim's point that "it appears that one way to increase the presence of women in institutions is through other women."[69]

CHALLENGES OF ALL-FEMALE POLICE UNITS

Even some feminist scholars are critical of all-women's police units because they see them as essentializing women as best to work with women. However, as Shannon Drysdale Walsh points out, such programs can create important change by offering specialized training for addressing crimes against women.[70] Also, by creating more opportunities for women to become security sector specialists, they counter essentialist views of women and challenge stereotypes of women as victims needing protection from men.[71]

At the same time, it is important to avoid rhetoric in support of FFPUs that draws on stereotypes and situates officers as "superheroines" whose capacity extends far beyond providing physical security in postconflict zones. FFPU members are often seen and indeed expected to bring many "extras" to the peacekeeping context above and beyond the provision of postconflict security, and these extras tend to involve carework that women are expected to be naturally more adept than men at providing. Yet while women living in zones where peacekeepers are deployed may be more likely to bring their claims to women officers, this is not necessarily because women peacekeepers are naturally more empathetic and open to their claims. Instead it may be because, unlike the men, women are *expected* to be more open to these claims. Additionally or alternatively it may be because as women these officers have experienced or witnessed gendered denials of justice that have made them more sensitive in responding to women.

While such issues have not been studied in depth in police peacekeeping, studies of military peace operations may be relevant. Laura Miller and Charles Moskos, in their research on American military members' perceptions of civilians in Somalia, found that although all soldiers were frustrated by some the behavior of locals, female and black male soldiers were more likely than white male soldiers to resist negative stereotyping and to seek to understand the locals as humans who were responding as anyone would to an awful situation.[72] The authors explain this resistance as based on personal experience of harmful gender or race stereotypes and consequently the feeling that stereotypes could unfairly dehumanize locals and entrench existing problems.[73] For similar reasons, as well as heightened expectations based on stereotypes, women police peacekeepers may be more likely to respond to crimes against local women. However, their doing so may also increase expectations of them and their workload or duration of deployment. For example, with regard to India's FFPU in Liberia, "What was supposed to be a six-month deployment was extended, because the female police officers were more willing to deal with the psychosocial effects of trauma."[74]

Given the obstacles to female peacekeeping service presented by mixed-gender units, the FFPU could usefully be understood as an alternative interpretation of gender mainstreaming, and perhaps at least initially conceived of as a temporary special measure. From this perspective, further FFPUs could be developed alongside existing efforts at increasing the gender integration of peacekeeping units. Increasing women's access to participation in peacekeeping will not be easy or happen overnight, but it is necessary. FFPUs appear to be one step in the right direction, though it is important to recognize that they cannot and should not be expected to solve all the problems women face when it comes to peace and security. Women are not some superpowered group naturally equipped to solve the problems blocking the way of peace. On the contrary, building sustainable peace will require work from both men and women, including peacekeepers, policy makers, humanitarian agency staff, members of community organizations, and the wider society.

Conclusion

Although the international community has paid increasing attention to the role of women in peace and security through the United Nations Security Council's Women, Peace and Security agenda and other related initiatives, many have suggested the need for "a little less talk, a lot more action." After all, progress toward more gender-equitable participation in the peace and security realm—particularly in peacekeeping operations—has been at times painfully slow. Within this context, gender mainstreaming has too often been interpreted loosely, differentially, or not at all. Furthermore, the dominant "gender-neutral" approach to peacekeeping can sometimes worsen women's position or marginalize important political discussion and action needed to improve women's status.

Following Cynthia Enloe's call for a feminist curiosity, this book set out to tell the story of the first FFPU deployed in UN peacekeeping. In doing so, it has looked at policies, attitudes, experiences, outcomes, and norms in seeking to better understand bigger questions of women, gender, peace, and security. This curiosity was sparked by the FFPU's emergence as a unique idea, policy, and practice that contributes a broader and more nuanced approach than many "typical" efforts of gender mainstreaming or implementing the UN's Women, Peace and Security agenda. As such, the FFPU is an interesting and valuable lens for considering theories and practice around gender equality in relation to security, political economy, and institutional cultures. Likewise, contributions made by the FFPU deserve more attention than they have received to date from scholars and policy makers. Understanding how the FFPU came about necessarily requires paying attention to strategies, channels of influence, and competing ideologies in both the domestic and global context. This book constitutes one step in that direction.

FFPUs can make significant contributions to the goals of gender equity, peace and security and can be driven and led by high-impact, elite actors with a personal interest in and commitment to these goals. By acting as norm entrepreneurs, both men and women at the UN and in the Indian state policing apparatus were able to conceive of, create, and deploy this first FFPU.

Once they hit the ground in Liberia, the FFPU showed themselves more than fit for their key responsibility of providing security in a postconflict context. Not only did they provide security for the community where they served, but they also challenged gender stereotypes that situate women as needing protection and as being incapable of providing protection. In doing so, they encouraged more local women to take on roles in the security sector, pursued greater use of nonlethal weapons, saw increased reporting and decreased incidents of sexual and gender-based violence, and shook up expectations by showing that in fact self-proclaimed "girls" and "mothers" can create secure environments as effectively as men, and in some circumstances perhaps even more effectively.

At the same time, the FFPU facilitated economic empowerment for women and girls by (1) helping to uphold the rights of women and girls— both to accessing security institutions and to participating in them, (2) supporting women's and girls' access to education, and (3) providing decent employment with comparatively high pay.

While receiving benefits from this work, the women of the FFPU were also expected to and did take on a "second shift" of volunteer community work. While many reported they enjoyed this work and found meaning in it, it is worth asking why women are expected to engage in such extra work and men in peacekeeping are not. Perhaps if male peacekeepers shared in this work, for example, the load for women peacekeepers would be reduced *and* male peacekeepers could gain more trust from communities and pride in the work they do. Overall, it is clear that states and international organizations like the UN can and should do more to increase women's involvement in peacekeeping by taking into account both the ways women may be marginalized from participation and the extra burdens of uncompensated "second shift" work they may carry compared to their male colleagues.

Those seeking to implement and expand this innovative policy and practice have faced a number of constraints. These have included many gendered fears incited by the FFPU's presence, including fears about women's presence in peacekeeping in general and women's participation in all-female units in particular. This second fear has been shown to reflect a limiting global culture of gender mainstreaming in peacekeeping that views women's involvement as "legitimate" or "appropriate" only when women participate as a small minority in male-majority units. However, these notions can and should be challenged.

Even if the UN does not feel the practice fits its long-term, idealistic vision for what gender equity should look like, FFPUs could arguably be understood as an alternative, worthwhile temporary special measure. As such, further FFPUs could be developed *alongside* existing efforts to increase gender integration in peacekeeping units. While continuing down the path to gender equity will require ongoing, challenging political work, these efforts are crucial. FFPUs appear to be one step in the right direction when used as part of a broader program that includes multiple ways of involving women rather than narrowly limiting their options to participating as members of a small minority in a male-dominated unit.

FFPUs should not be expected to solve all the problems women face when it comes to peace and security. Indeed, significant shifts are needed away from both stereotypes that say women cannot or should not provide security and those that situate women peacekeepers as superheroines who are naturally adept at peacebuilding. Instead, what is needed is difficult but rewarding work by men, women, peacekeepers, policy makers, and the broader society to think better and more deeply around what women's participation in peacekeeping can mean. The superheroine narrative, which is implicit in the dominant instrumentalist claims regarding services that female peacekeepers provide "freely" and "naturally," can lead to unrealistic expectations of what women can do, as individuals or within a group. Beyond being unfair to the women involved, this can actually hinder their abilities to protect and serve—which is after all their primary job as peacekeepers.

Despite facing many challenges, the FFPU has continued to represent a unique, action-oriented approach, giving legitimacy to women's needs and concerns both as stakeholders in peace and security processes and as active peacekeepers. Overall, the FFPU appears to be a potentially transformative, yet simultaneously pragmatic policy. To be clear, the aim here is *not* to suggest that the policies and practices associated with the FFPU are better for *all* women everywhere but rather to suggest that they may pose a good and fair option for many women in many contexts and thus deserve fair consideration as part of a broader Women, Peace and Security program.

The commonly held assumption that women globally are a homogeneous group is not only inaccurate but potentially harmful for women and detrimental to the goals of achieving gender equity in peace and security initiatives and more generally. At the same time, as Chandra Mohanty argues, "In knowing differences and particularities, we can better see the connections and commonalities because no border or boundary is ever complete or rigidly determining. The challenge is to see how differences allow us to explain the connections and border crossings better and more accurately."[1] Mohanty calls for particularized, grounded analyses that pay attention to global political and economic frameworks,[2] as this book has sought to do, while recognizing that "the local and the global are not defined in terms of physical geography or territory but exist simultaneously and constitute each other."[3]

While this book has taken significant steps toward filling existing gaps in the research, further critical analysis of the deployment of FFPUs is needed to explore the impacts on the women peacekeepers themselves as well as on women living in conflict zones where women peacekeepers are present. Key future research questions might include, but need not be limited to:

- How (if at all) has the international attention to the Indian FFPU influenced prospects for women back home in the Indian policing context?

- Does this case support the argument for quota systems, single-sex systems, or both in policing more broadly?
- What have been the outcomes for officers returning from FFPU duty?
- What might differ for female peacekeepers in an all-female environment compared to one with both male and female peacekeepers?
- Are there reported changes in values and beliefs around gender norms as they relate to issues of peace and security in the deploying country or the host country?
- How might other factors that intersect with gender—such as race, class, and religion—affect prospects for women in peacekeeping?
- How might these factors affect relations between female peacekeepers and local women?
- How have the other FFPUs deployed by Bangladesh fared in their roles in UN peacekeeping?
- How might their experiences and outcomes differ from those of the Indian contingent and why?
- How have other FFPUs affected the prevalence and prosecution of sexual and gender-based violence?
- How do local populations in the mission host countries perceive women peacekeepers?
- Does this differ across countries of deployment?
- Does it differ between places hosting FFPUs and places hosting women officers as a small minority in male-majority contingents? If so, how and why?
- Does the presence of FFPUs in particular or women peacekeepers in general affect perceptions of security in local populations? If so, how and why?
- What does the FFPU's story mean in the longer term? Is there potential for institutionalization? If so, what dangers or prospects would this pose domestically and internationally?

Although fairly extensive, this list of questions is merely a starting point for what I hope will be even broader-ranging opportunities for research, discussion, and collaboration. Better understanding the issues presented here around women, peace and security will necessarily involve ongoing and crucial work by scholars, humanitarian agency staff, members of community organizations, policy makers, and activists. While the relatively small-scale deployment of all-female units may change the way women are perceived and their roles constructed in peace and security, it is important to remember that perceptions do not occur in a power vacuum devoid of gender norms and are necessarily affected by the way gender is constituted both locally and globally.

For now, this case shows that significant and innovative changes can happen, even within conservative institutions beholden to a variety of stakeholders, not all of whom support women's participation in peace and security. Moreover, while there are still many impediments to adequately implementing gender perspectives in peacekeeping, it appears that the situation now is riper for change than it ever has been. In the words of Indian author and activist Arundhati Roy, "Another world is not only possible. She is on her way. On a quiet day, I can hear her breathing."[4]

APPENDIX Interviews

Interviews were conducted in New York and Washington, D.C. (USA) from September to October 2012, in Delhi (India) in October 2013, and in Monrovia (Liberia) from February to March 2014, as well as via Skype and telephone throughout the project duration. Interviewees included

Four current (as of September/October 2012) UN employees working in New York on peacekeeping who wish to remain anonymous

A former formed police unit (FPU) coordinator for the UN Mission in Liberia (UNMIL) who was working in this capacity in Liberia during the introduction of the first all-female formed police unit (FFPU) and during the second group's arrival

Three former UN police advisers

A former UN special envoy (special representative to the secretary general) who was in Liberia from 2008 to 2012

Two former FFPU commanders, both of whom have returned to duties with the Central Reserve Police Force

One former senior official in Indian peacekeeping policy

One official from the research office of the Indian Police Service

Two Indian scholars whose work focuses on women in policing in India

The UN Police Division (UNPOL) police commissioner in UNMIL

The FPU coordinator in UNMIL

The FFPU commander (India) in UNMIL

An FFPU officer in UNMIL

A female UNPOL officer (US) in UNMIL

A female UNPOL officer (UK) in UNMIL

Two female UNPOL officers (Bosnia) in UNMIL

A female UNPOL officer (Ukraine) in UNMIL

Two female UNPOL officers/regional commanders (Sweden) in UNMIL

An Office of the Gender Advisor representative in UNMIL

A special representative to the secretary general representative in UNMIL

A UN Women representative in UNMIL

Questions included topics such as:

- How the idea for the all-female formed police unit (FFPU) had emerged and how the process of turning it into a reality occurred
- Whether/what benefits were expected from or were thought to have occurred because of the introduction of the FFPU
- What (if any) ways interviewees thought the FFPU might benefit women
- What kinds of work the FFPU were/had been doing, and whether that work differed from work by colleagues in all-male or mixed-gender contingents
- Whether any research had been done through the UN on the outcomes of the FFPU, and whether any research I conducted could be adapted to provide useful outcomes for the UN

Notes

INTRODUCTION

1. Khosa, "CRPF's Mahila Battalion."

2. "UN Envoy."

3. Anderholt, "Female Participation," 37–38.

4. United Nations Department of Peacekeeping Operations, *Background Note;* United Nations Department of Public Information, "Female Police"; Pruitt, "All-Female Police Contingents"; United Nations News Centre, "UN Peacekeeping."

5. Karame, "Military Women"; DeGroot, "Few Good Women"; Mazurana, "Do Women Matter."

6. Jennings, "Protecting Whom?"; Bridges and Horsfall, "Increasing Operational Effectiveness"; Harris and Goldsmith, "Gendering Transnational Policing"; Sion, "Peacekeeping"; Henry, "Peacexploitation?"

7. Tickner, *Feminist Voyage,* 97.

8. Theidon and Phenicie, *Gender, Conflict, and Peacebuilding,* 9.

9. Anderholt, "Female Participation," 1. Important related work has also been done on women's roles in peacebuilding; see, e.g., Anderlini, *Women Building Peace.* Related work has also been done on women's roles in soldiering; see MacKenzie, *Female Soldiers.*

10. Theidon and Phenicie, *Gender, Conflict, and Peacebuilding,* 14.

11. Sjoberg, *Gender War, and Conflict,* 8.

12. Tickner, *Feminist Voyage,* 94.

13. Ibid.

14. Robert W. Cox, "Social Forces, States and World Orders: Beyond International Relations Theory," *Millennium: Journal of International Studies* 10 (1981): 129–30, cited in Tickner, *Feminist Voyage*, 83.

15. Tickner, *Feminist Voyage*, 83.

16. Kronsell, "Methods for Studying Silences," 119; H. Hudson, "Peacekeeping Trends," 804.

17. Hautzinger, *Violence in the City*, 255.

18. Enloe, *Seriously!* 17.

19. Tickner, *Feminist Voyage*, 25.

20. Walker, *Moral Understandings*, 81.

21. Rubinstein, "Methodological Challenges," 138.

22. Nader, "Up the Anthropologist"; Nader, "Key Note Address."

23. Bowman, "Studying Up."

24. Rubinstein, "Methodological Challenges," 144.

25. Kronsell, "Methods for Studying Silences," 122.

26. Liebowitz and Zwingel, "Gender Equality Oversimplified," 378.

27. Chapter 6 does include some quotes and analysis from interviews I was able to do with women serving in mixed-gender contexts as individual police officers in UNMIL.

28. Olsson, Schjølset, and Möller, "Women's Participation," 38.

29. Ibid., 55.

30. N. Hudson and Goetz, "Too Much," 339.

31. A more detailed discussion of Resolution 1325 and the WPS agenda, including information on origins and debates, is included in chapter 1.

32. Whitworth, *Men;* Gibbings, "No Angry Women," 535.

33. Olsson, "Namibian Peace Operation," 168.

1. THE FFPU IN A GLOBAL CONTEXT

1. Rubinstein, "Methodological Challenges," 139.

2. Conaway and Shoemaker, *Women.*

3. Olsson and Gizelis, "Introduction to Resolution 1325," 3–4.

4. Mazurana, Raven-Roberts, and Parpart, Introduction to Mazurana, Raven-Roberts, and Parpart, *Gender, Conflict, and Peacekeeping*, 19.

5. Ibid.; Rubinstein, "Methodological Challenges," 139.

6. Greener, "UNPOL," 106.

7. Grabosky, "Police as International Peacekeepers," 101.

8. Anderholt, "Female Participation," 4.

9. Ibid.

10. Grabosky, "Police as International Peacekeepers," 101.

11. Beede, "Roles of Paramilitary," 54.

12. Andrade, *World Police*, xi.

13. Beede, "Roles of Paramilitary," 54.

14. Ibid., 53.

15. Ibid.

16. Anderholt, "Female Participation," 6.

17. Ibid., iii.

18. Ibid., 2.

19. Ibid.

20. Ibid., 2–3.

21. Harrington, "Resolution 1325," 566.

22. Haas and Schäfer, "Masculinity and Civil Wars."

23. de la Rey and McKay, "Peacebuilding"; Karam, "Women in War"; Gender and Peacebuilding Working Group, "Fact Sheet: Resolution 1325"; Pankhurst, "'Sex War'"; Porter, "Women."

24. Raven-Roberts, "Women," 36.

25. Sjoberg, *Gender, War, and Conflict*, 3.

26. Kronsell, "Methods for Studying Silences," 111.

27. Ibid., 108; Connell, *Masculinities*, 77.

28. Hays, "Structure and Agency," 65.

29. Ibid.

30. Ibid.

31. Ibid.

32. Jennings, "Service, Sex and Security,"326.

33. Kronsell, "Methods for Studying Silences," 109.

34. See Siebold, "Core Issues," 149, for an example of such an approach to the military.

35. Ibid., 146.

36. Cohn and Jacobson, "Women and Political Activism," 113.

37. Ibid.

38. Theidon and Phenicie, *Gender, Conflict, and Peacebuilding*, 12.

39. Tickner, *Feminist Voyage*, 76.

40. Liebowitz and Zwingel, "Gender Equality Oversimplified," 367.

41. Theidon and Phenicie, *Gender, Conflict, and Peacebuilding*, 15.

42. Liebowitz and Zwingel, "Gender Equality Oversimplified," 380.

43. Harrington, "Resolution 1325," 567.

44. Kronsell, "Methods for Studying Silences," 112.

45. J. Acker, "Hierarchies, Jobs, Bodies: A Theory of Gendered Organizations," Gender and Society 4 (1990): 139–58, Cynthia Cockburn, *In the Way of Women: Men's Resistance to Sex Equality in Organizations* (London: Zed, 1991), and A. Rao and R. Stuart, "Rethinking Organisations: A Feminist Perspective," *Gender and Development* 5 (1997): 10–16, all cited in True and Mintrom, "Transnational Networks," 44.

46. Jacobson, "Women 'after' Wars," 232.

47. Hautzinger, *Violence in the City,* 221.

48. Ibid., 255.

49. Ibid., 194.

50. Ibid., 263, 267.

51. Ibid., 229, 231.

52. Banerjee, "India," 237.

53. Henry, "Peacexploitation?," 18.

54. Ibid., 26.

55. Ibid.; *All Girl Squad.*

56. For more a more detailed exploration of the lead-up to the passage of Resolution 1325, see N. Hudson, "En-gendering UN Peacekeeping Operations."

57. Shepherd, "Sex, Security and Superhero(in)es," 505. For a more detailed analysis of the implementation of Resolution 1325 to date, see Gizelis and Olsson, *Gender, Peace and Security.*

58. Shepherd, "Sex, Security, and Superhero(in)es," 505.

59. Davies, "Pursuing Women's Peace," 547; Tryggestad, "UN Peacebuilding Commission."

60. H. Hudson, "Peacekeeping Trends," 790.

61. United Nations Security Council, "Women, Peace and Security,"1.

62. H. Hudson, "Peacekeeping Trends," 112.

63. Pankhurst, "'Sex War," 153; Porter, "Women," 248.

64. Gender and Peacebuilding Working Group, "Fact Sheet: Understanding."

65. Pruitt, "Women, Peace and Security Agenda."

66. Vlachova and Biason, *Women.*

67. United Nations Peacekeeping, "Fact Sheet."

68. Ivanovic, "Why."

69. United Nations Peacekeeping, "Gender Statistics." See also United Nations Security Council, Resolution 1820; Global Action, "Security Council Open Debate"; Rubinstein, *Peacekeeping under Fire,* 14. Women also participate in peacekeeping outside the UN—for example, through EU and NATO missions. See Olsson, Schjølset, and Möller, "Women's Participation."

70. United Nations Department of Peacekeeping Operations, "WANTED Skilled Police Officers," 11.

71. Olsson, Schjølset, and Möller, "Women's Participation," 48.

72. United Nations Peacekeeping, "Policy Dialogue," 3.

73. Ford, "UN Passes New Resolution."

74. Anderholt, "Female Participation," 36.

75. United Nations Mission in Liberia, "Gender Mainstreaming," 3.

76. Ibid.

77. Ibid., 43.

78. Ibid., 4.

79. Gbowee, *Mighty Be Our Powers.*

80. United Nations Mission in Liberia, "Gender Mainstreaming," 4.

81. Anderholt, "Female Participation," 36.

82. Sirleaf, *This Child,* 305.

83. H. Hudson, "Peacekeeping Trends," 799.

84. Ibid.

85. United Nations Mission in Liberia, "Gender Mainstreaming," 4.

86. Ibid.

87. Durch et al., *Understanding Impact of Police.*

88. Dunn, "'You Will Go Far.'"

89. Ibid.

90. United Nations Mission in Liberia, "Gender Mainstreaming," 5

91. Naughtie, "Liberia."

92. United Nations Mission in Liberia, "Gender Mainstreaming," 5.

93. Sirleaf, *Speech by Ellen Johnson-Sirleaf.*

94. Dunn, "'You Will Go Far.'"

2. HOW THE FFPU BEGAN

1. In terms of procedure, the DPKO normally poses troop requests for peacekeeping to the Indian Permanent Mission (PMI) in the New York UN office, and the PMI then conveys the request to the Ministry of External Affairs, which is located in Delhi. For more on this process, see Banerjee, *Providing Peacekeepers,* 237.

2. Narayan, "Cross-cultural Connections," 66. This may be particularly significant in terms of translating local initiatives into international practices like the FFPU. As Anne Marie Goetz, formerly chief adviser to Peace and Security for UN Women, has argued that "in the long run, the only thing that is going to change international policy is the strength of the domestic women's movement in any specific country, and that change coming through that country to the international arena." See N. Hudson and Goetz, "Too Much," 341.

3. Narayan, "Cross-cultural Connections," 64; Katzenstein, "Organizing against Violence."

4. Narayan, "Cross-cultural Connections," 64; Katzenstein, "Organizing against Violence."

5. Beath, Fotini, and Enikolopov, "Empowering Women," 541.

6. "India Approves Rule"; Young, "Women on the Beat."

7. Aleem, "Women in Policing."

8. Ibid.

9. Hautzinger, *Violence in the City,* 182, puts the date at 1973.

10. Isaac and Tharakan, "Kerala," 1994.

11. Ibid., 1995; Narayan, "Cross-cultural Connections," 72.

12. Isaac and Tharakan, "Kerala," 2001.

13. Ibid. While Kerala is in South India, local conditions in other areas have also facilitated gender relations that challenge dominant assumptions. For example, Singhal notes that in parts of northeastern India men are seen as homemakers while women are wage earners. See Singhal, "Women, Gender and Development," 175.

14. Shekhar and Lord, "Women Police," 4.

15. Hautzinger, *Violence in the City*, 183.

16. Shekhar and Lord, "Women Police," 4–5.

17. Ibid.

18. Ibid.

19. Ibid., 5.

20. Ibid., 4–5.

21. Hautzinger, *Violence in the City*, 183.

22. Shekhar and Lord, "Women Police," 5.

23. Ibid., 10.

24. Bhagavathy and Shekhar, "Access to Justice," 103; Kethineni and Srinivasan, "Police Handling."

25. M. Natarajan, "Women Police Stations as a Dispute Processing System," *Women and Criminal Justice* 16, nos. 1–2 (2005): 103, cited in Kethineni and Srinivasan, "Police Handling," 211.

26. Hautzinger, *Violence in the City*, 211.

27. C. MacDowell Santos, "Engendering the Police: Women's Police Stations and Feminism in Sao Paulo," *Latin American Research Review* 39, no. 3: 29–55, cited in Walsh, "Engendering Justice," 51.

28. Hautzinger, *Violence in the City*, 212.

29. Shekhar and Lord, "Women Police," 5, 8. Similar outcomes were found in research on Brazil's AWPSs: policewomen faced discrimination from male police, who saw the creation of AWPSs "as a loss of turf" and thus disrespected the women's police stations, refused to patrol with women, spread sexual rumors about the policewomen, and removed women from cases because of stereotypical notions that they could not be tough enough or sufficiently qualified. Furthermore, controversy over sex-segregated policing approaches has continued over the years. See Hautzinger, *Violence in the City*, 201, 243.

30. Shekhar and Lord, "Women Police," 4–5.

31. M. Natarajan, "Women Police in Tamil Nadu, India: A Tale of Two Cohorts," *International Journal of Comparative Criminology* 2, no. 2 (2002): 201–24, cited in Shekhar and Lord, "Women Police," 4–5.

32. Shekhar and Lord, "Women Police," 7.

33. Bhagavathy and Shekhar, "Access to Justice," 103; Natarajan, "Women Police Units."

34. Shekhar and Lord, "Women Police," 10.

35. Tickner, *Feminist Voyage*, 145.

36. James N. Rosenau, *Along the Domestic-Foreign Frontier: Exploring Governance in a Turbulent World* (Cambridge: Cambridge University Press, 1997), cited in True and Mintrom, "Transnational Networks," 29.

37. Banerjee, "India," 243.

38. Ibid., 238.

39. Gowan and Singh, "India and UN Peacekeeping," 177.

40. Ibid.

41. Banerjee, "India," 227.

42. Gowan and Singh, "India and UN Peacekeeping," 183.

43. Ibid.

44. Ibid., 178, 184.

45. Ibid., 190.

46. Krishnasamy, "Case for India's 'Leadership,'" 225.

47. Dharmapuri, "Just Add Women," 56.

48. See WILPF's PeaceWomen website at www.peacewomen.org/member-states for an updated list.

49. For other examples from Latin America, see Walsh, "Engendering Justice," 251.

50. True and Mintrom, "Transnational Networks," 28.

51. Gowan and Singh, "India and UN Peacekeeping," 177.

52. Hautzinger, *Violence in the City,* 187.

53. Gowan and Singh, "India and UN Peacekeeping," 187.

54. Banerjee, "India," 227.

55. Gowan and Singh, "India and UN Peacekeeping," 180.

56. Banerjee, "India," 240.

57. Pruitt, "All-Female Police Contingents."

58. Gowan and Singh, "India and UN Peacekeeping," 178.

59. Banerjee, "India," 225.

60. Gowan and Singh, "India and UN Peacekeeping," 182.

61. Ibid., 184.

62. Jennings, "Service, Sex and Security," 326.

63. Tickner, *Feminist Voyage,* 26.

64. Sjoberg, *Gender, War, and Conflict,* 49.

65. Cohn, "Women and Wars," 19.

66. Walsh, "Engendering Justice," 58.

67. Shekhar and Lord, "Women Police," 5.

3. WOMEN AT WORK

1. Tickner, *Feminist Voyage,* 46.

2. "Woman Who Took On Zimbabwe's Security Men."

3. Cordell, "Liberia Women Peacekeepers."

4. Jennings, "Service, Sex and Security," 324.

5. Tickner, *Feminist Voyage*, 46.

6. Cordell, "Liberia Women Peacekeepers."

7. Ibid.

8. Anderholt, "Female Participation," 39.

9. True, *Political Economy of Violence*, 152.

10. Hautzinger, *Violence in the City*, 182.

11. Ibid., 184.

12. Ibid., 183.

13. Ibid., 214.

14. Ibid., 184.

15. Jubb et al., "Regional Mapping Study"; Hautzinger, *Violence in the City;* Walsh, "Engendering Justice."

16. Hautzinger, *Violence in the City*, 216.

17. Ibid., 137, 91.

18. Merry, "Rights Talk," 381.

19. Ibid., 347, 343.

20. Hautzinger, *Violence in the City*, 92.

21. Walsh, "Engendering Justice," 49.

22. Goodale and Merry, *Practice of Human Rights*, 4.

23. Sion, "Peacekeeping."

24. This study referred to English-language resources, which limited the scope of data available, given that India is home to hundreds of languages, with Hindi being the first official language and English the secondary official language. Nevertheless, "More Indians speak English than any other language, with the sole exception of Hindi' ("Indiaspeak"). Future research could include other languages as well as Liberian and international discourse around the Indian FFPU.

25. "All-Women Unit."

26. Khosa, "CRPF's Mahila Battalion."

27. "All-Women Unit."

28. "RAF Deploys Women"; "Commander of All-Female Indian Police Unit"; Aziz, "Keepers of Peace."

29. Aziz, "Keepers of Peace."

30. "Tharoor on a Six-Day Visit"; "CRPF's All-Women Team"; Aziz, "Keepers of Peace."

31. A. Sharma, "UN Showers Praise."

32. "Indian Female Police Officers."

33. Thakur, "Unintended Consequences."

34. "India to Send."

35. Shourie, "First All-Women UN Peacekeeping Unit"; "Indian Female Blue Berets."

36. Aziz, "Keepers of Peace."

37. Cited in B. Sharma, "Indian Women Peacekeepers."

38. A. Sharma, "UN Showers Praise."

39. Ibid.

40. "New Mandates"; "Indian Female Police Unit."

41. "India Seeks Greater Role."

42. "New Mandates."

43. "Indian Female Police Unit."

44. Simić, "Does the Presence of Women Really Matter?"

45. United Nations Mission in Liberia, "Gender Mainstreaming," 44.

46. Ibid.

47. Ibid.

48. Ibid., viii.

49. Ibid., 40.

50. Ibid., 41.

51. Anderholt, "Female Participation," 38, 39; Karim, "Do Gender Balancing Policies," 41.

52. United Nations Mission in Liberia, "Gender Mainstreaming," 42.

53. de Alwis, Mertus, and Sajjad, "Women and Peace Processes," 185–86.

54. Cordell, "Liberia Women Peacekeepers."

55. Lea Biason, quoted in Anderholt, "Female Participation," 38.

56. Harris, "Sustainable Development," 183.

57. "Women on Top," emphasis added.

58. A. Sharma, "UN Showers Praise," emphasis added.

59. Ibid.

60. "UNGA President."

61. de Alwis, Mertus, and Sajjad, "Women and Peace Processes," 176.

62. Mazurana, "Women, Girls," 157; de Alwis, Mertus, and Sajjad, "Women and Peace Processes."

63. de Alwis, Mertus, and Sajjad, "Women and Peace Processes," 176.

64. Ibid.

65. Lopes, "Militarized Masculinity," 16.

66. Rubinstein, *Peacekeeping under Fire*, 101.

67. Hautzinger, *Violence in the City*, 198, 193.

68. Ibid., 222.

69. Ibid., 223.

70. Ibid., 225.

71. Ibid., 207.

72. Ibid., 217.

73. Beardsley et al., "Gender Balancing," 4.

74. Some policewomen in Brazil, for example, have argued that states should not be "letting male police off the hook," suggesting that instead they too should

be trained and equipped to play valuable roles in reducing violence against women. At the same time, these women still see the need for women-run police stations, and none would like to see men leading those stations. See Hautzinger, *Violence in the City*, 267.

75. Beardsley et al., "Gender Balancing."

76. True, *Political Economy of Violence*, 35. See also Flood, "Why Violence"; Katz, *Macho Paradox*.

4. POLITICAL ECONOMY, WOMEN, AND PEACEKEEPING

1. Sjoberg, *Gender, War, and Conflict;* True, *Political Economy of Violence;* Tickner, *Feminist Voyage;* Meger, "Toward a Feminist Political Economy"; Jennings, "Service, Sex and Security"; Enloe, *Seriously!* Important work theorizing around the need for linking feminist efforts with a political economic analysis more generally can also be found in Mohanty's work. See Mohanty, "'Under Western Eyes' Revisited." Further work on incorporating a gendered analysis in considering approaches to women's economic participation can also be found in Rankin's work. See Rankin, "Governing Development."

2. Sjoberg, *Gender, War, and Conflict;* True, *Political Economy of Violence;* Tickner, *Feminist Voyage;* Cohn, "Women and Wars."

3. Tickner, *Feminist Voyage*, 46, 34.

4. Sjoberg, *Gender, War, and Conflict*, 34.

5. Tickner, *Feminist Voyage*, 64.

6. True, *Political Economy of Violence*.

7. Sjoberg, *Gender, War, and Conflict*, 131.

8. Harris, "Sustainable Development Following Conflicts," 184.

9. Enloe, *Seriously!*, 110.

10. True, *Political Economy of Violence*, 5.

11. Ibid., 188.

12. Chang, "Role of Social Policy," 248.

13. Olsson and Gizelis, "Introduction to Resolution 1325," 12.

14. N. Hudson and Goetz, "Too Much," 337.

15. True, *Political Economy of Violence*, 28.

16. Hautzinger, *Violence in the City*, 234.

17. True, *Political Economy of Violence;* Rankin, "Governing Development."

18. Jennings, "Service, Sex and Security," 326.

19. Beath, Fotini, and Enikolopov, "Empowering Women," 555, 540–41.

20. Ibid., 549.

21. Ibid., 553.

22. Kabeer, Khan, and Adlparvar, "Afghan Values," 3.

23. Ibid., 31.

24. Ibid., 25–26.

25. Ibid., 3, 9.

26. Beath, Fotini, and Enikolopov, "Empowering Women," 540–541.

27. Bhavnani, "Do Electoral Quotas Work?," cited in Beath, Fotini, and Enikolopov, "Empowering Women," 541; Beath, Fotini, and Enikolopov, "Empowering Women," 545.

28. Beath, Fotini, and Enikolopov, "Empowering Women," 556.

29. Enloe, *Curious Feminist*, 20.

30. Cohn, Kinsella, and Gibbins, "Women, Peace and Security" (roundtable of six participants), 136.

31. Mathers, "Women and State Military Forces," 126.

32. Jennings, "Service, Sex and Security," 314.

33. Pupavac, "Empowering Women?"

34. Karim and Beardsley, "Female Peacekeepers," 467.

35. Ibid., 467.

36. Henry, "Peacexploitation?," 20.

37. UN police staff member, interview, New York, October 2, 2012.

38. Rubinstein, *Peacekeeping under Fire*, 55.

39. Avantika and Saxena, "Study of Career Drivers."

40. Shekhar and Lord, "Women Police," 7.

41. Ibid., 8.

42. Mathers, "Women," 134.

43. N. Hudson and Goetz, "Too Much," 342.

44. Cordell, "Liberia Women Peacekeepers"; King and Theliander, "Indian Formed Police Unit," 10.

45. Allen, "Liberia."

46. Olsson, Schjølset, and Möller, "Women's Participation," 45.

47. Ibid.

48. This added expectation may been seen as coming from the way women's involvement has been "sold" by the UN as "naturally" bringing such "bonus" outcomes, but it is possible that some women may also place this expectation on themselves and their colleagues, either because they feel this is a "natural" obligation of women or because it is necessary to uphold the positive image of women in peacekeeping, which has often relied on this instrumentalized framework.

49. Hautzinger, *Violence in the City*, 242.

50. Ibid., 195.

51. Ibid., 207.

52. Cohn, Kinsella, and Gibbins, "Women, Peace and Security," 136.

53. Jennings, "Women's Participation," 8.

54. Ibid., 8.

55. Sion, "Peacekeeping," 562.

56. Ibid.

57. Raven-Roberts, "Gender Mainstreaming," 54.

58. Mathers, "Women."

59. Henry, 'Peacexploitation?," 26; *All Girl Squad*.

60. Khosa, "CRPF's Mahila Battalion"; Bhasin, "These CRPF Cops."

61. Jennings, "Women's Participation," 8.

62. Ibid.

63. Olsson and Gizelis, "Introduction to Resolution 1325," 5.

64. Ibid., 2.

65. N. Hudson, "Securitizing Women's Rights," 59.

66. N. Hudson and Goetz, "Too Much," 342.

67. Karim and Beardsley, "Female Peacekeepers," 465; United Nations Peacekeeping, "Policy Dialogue."

68. United Nations Mission in Liberia, "Gender Mainstreaming," 39.

69. Bridges and Horsfall, "Increasing Operational Effectiveness."

70. Kirshenbaum, "In U.N. Peacekeeping."

71. United Nations Peacekeeping, "Women in Peacekeeping."

72. "Women UN Peacekeepers."

73. Jennings, "Women's Participation," 4.

74. Gibbings, "No Angry Women," 525, 527.

75. Ibid., 529.

76. de Alwis, Mertus, and Sajjad, "Women and Peace Processes," 186.

77. Karim, "Do Gender Balancing Policies," 9, 10, 18.

78. Theidon and Phenicie, *Gender, Conflict, and Peacebuilding*, 6.

79. de Alwis, Mertus, and Sajjad, "Women and Peace Processes," 192.

80. Enloe, *Seriously!*, 16.

81. Ibid.

82. Anderholt, "Female Participation," 50.

83. Jennings, "Service, Sex and Security," 314.

84. Ibid., 315.

85. Ibid.

86. Rubinstein, *Peacekeeping under Fire*, 120.

87. Ibid.

88. Jennings, "Service, Sex and Security," 316.

89. United Nations Mission in Liberia, "Gender Mainstreaming," 24.

90. Ibid.

91. Ibid., 20, 21.

92. Ibid., 19, 20.

93. Ibid., 21.

94. Beardsley et al., "Gender Balancing," 2.

95. Cordell, "Liberia Women Peacekeepers."

96. Ibid.

97. United Nations Peacekeeping, "Policy Dialogue," 3.
98. Karim and Beardsley, "Female Peacekeepers," 484.
99. Jennings, "Service, Sex and Security," 314.
100. Mathers, "Women," 128.
101. Cohn, Kinsella, and Gibbins, "Women, Peace and Security," 136.

5. WHO'S AFRAID OF THE GIRLS?

1. Jacobson, "Women 'after' Wars," 223.
2. These barriers are explored in more detail in the next chapter.
3. Rubinstein, *Peacekeeping under Fire*.
4. Hays, "Structure and Agency," 68 (italics in original).
5. Rubinstein, *Peacekeeping under Fire*, 52.
6. Paris, "Peacekeeping," 441–43.
7. Ibid., 441, 443.
8. March and Olsen, "Institutional Dynamics," 952.
9. Paris, "Peacekeeping," 444.
10. Walsh, "Engendering Justice." See also Keck and Sikkink, *Activists beyond Borders*, 18, on "accountability politics."
11. Paris, "Peacekeeping," 461.
12. N. Hudson and Goetz, "Too Much," 341.
13. Paris, "Peacekeeping," 462.
14. Ibid., 463.
15. Ibid., 451.
16. Segal, "Women's Military Roles," 758.
17. Ibid., 769.
18. Ibid.
19. Ibid.
20. Kronsell, "Methods for Studying Silences," 109.
21. However, as Natalie Hudson notes, "The concept . . . has been important, although often misunderstood, in development policy circles since the 1970s." N. Hudson, "En-gendering UN Peacekeeping Operations," 794.
22. True and Mintrom, "Transnational Networks," 31.
23. Ibid., 33.
24. Ibid., 31; Joachim and Schneiker, "Changing Discourses."
25. Beardsley et al., "Gender Balancing," 4.
26. Mazurana, Raven-Roberts, and Parpart, introduction to Mazurana, Raven-Roberts, and Parpart, *Gender, Conflict, and Peacekeeping*.
27. Karim, "Do Gender Balancing Policies," 8.
28. Theidon and Phenicie, *Gender, Conflict, and Peacebuilding*, 10.
29. Ibid.

30. True and Mintrom, "Transnational Networks," 33.

31. Theidon and Phenicie, *Gender, Conflict, and Peacebuilding,* 10.

32. Whitworth, *Men.*

33. Basini, "Gender Mainstreaming Unraveled."

34. Charlesworth, "Not Waving but Drowning."

35. Joachim and Schneiker, "Changing Discourses"; Olsson and Gizelis, "Introduction to Resolution 1325," 10.

36. Joachim and Schneiker, "Changing Discourses."

37. Hautzinger, *Violence in the City,* 215.

38. Ibid., 185.

39. Ibid.

40. de Alwis, Mertus, and Sajjad, "Women and Peace Processes," 177–78.

41. Ibid.

42. Raven-Roberts, "Gender Mainstreaming," 44.

43. Ibid., 53.

44. Ibid.

45. United Nations Peacekeeping, "Policy Dialogue," 11.

46. Enloe, *Curious Feminist,* 199.

47. Theidon and Phenicie, *Gender, Conflict, and Peacebuilding,* 12.

48. Merry, "Rights Talk," 359.

49. Narayan, "Cross-cultural Connections," 64.

50. Goodale and Merry, *Practice of Human Rights,* 2.

51. Narayan, "Cross-cultural Connections," 65; Kishwar, "Why I Do Not."

52. Narayan, "Cross-cultural Connections," 66; Kishwar, "Why I Do Not."

53. Narayan, "Cross-cultural Connections," 66; Kishwar, "Why I Do Not."

54. Narayan, "Cross-cultural Connections," 66, 68.

55. Ibid., 68, 69.

56. Ibid., 70.

57. Ibid.

58. Anderholt, "Female Participation."

59. Poole, "Institutional Change"; Poole, "The World Is Outraged."

6. INCREASING WOMEN'S PARTICIPATION IN PEACE AND SECURITY

1. See, *inter alia,* DeGroot, "Few Good Women."

2. Anderholt, "Female Participation," 15.

3. Allred, "Peacekeepers and Prostitutes."

4. Anderholt, "Female Participation," 15.

5. Simić, "Does the Presence of Women Really Matter?," 188.

6. "Women UN Peacekeepers."

7. Merry, "Rights Talk," 379.

8. Rubinstein, *Peacekeeping under Fire*, 14.

9. Skjelsbaek, "Sexual Violence," 81.

10. Vlachova and Biason, *Women;* Harris and Goldsmith, "Gendering Transnational Policing"; Rehn and Sirleaf, *Women, War and Peace*. Moreover, one expected outcome of women's police stations in Brazil was that having all-female staff would avoid the common bias of male police minimizing or ignoring women's complaints, blaming women complainants, and overall not taking their complaints seriously. It was hoped that women police would identify more with their fellow women and experience empathy with their plights, rather than further victimizing them. Unprecedented recording of gender-based crimes has occurred, and prosecution and conviction rates for these offenses have risen significantly, though the rates remain unsatisfactory. See Hautzinger, *Violence in the City*, 2, 137, 187.

11. Beardsley et al., "Gender Balancing," 7; Meier and Nicholson-Crotty, "Gender."

12. "UN Seeks More Female Peacekeepers."

13. "Women UN Peacekeepers."

14. Steinberg, "Beyond Victimhood"; Conaway, *Role of Women;* International Crisis Group, "Congo"; United Nations Department of Political Affairs et al., "Conflict Related Sexual Violence."

15. Beardsley et al., "Gender Balancing," 23.

16. Ibid., 7.

17. Ofori, "Call," 1.

18. Ibid.

19. Ospina, *Ten-Year Impact Study*, 25.

20. Ibid.

21. Ibid., 10.

22. Jacobson, "Women 'after' Wars," 222.

23. Anderholt, "Female Participation," 44.

24. Ibid., 45.

25. DeGroot, "Few Good Women."

26. Ospina, *Ten-Year Impact Study*, 10.

27. Woolsey, "Challenges for Women," 78.

28. Alaga and Birikorang, "Security Sector Reform."

29. United Nations Mission in Liberia, "Gender Mainstreaming," 23.

30. Hautzinger, *Violence in the City*, 138.

31. Schjølset, *NATO and the Women*.

32. Stiehm, "Women, Peacekeeping and Peacemaking."

33. Bedi, *I Dare!*, 285.

34. Anderholt, "Female Participation," 44, 46.

35. Ibid., 46.

36. United Nations Department of Peacekeeping Operations, "WANTED Skilled Police Officers," 11.

37. Conaway and Shoemaker, "Women in United Nations."

38. Pruitt, "Looking Back."

39. United Nations Department of Peacekeeping Operations, "WANTED Skilled Police Officers," 11.

40. Ibid.

41. H. Hudson, "Peacekeeping Trends," 112.

42. Simić, "Does the Presence of Women Really Matter?"

43. Karame, "Military Women."

44. Jennings, "Protecting Whom?"

45. Ibid.

46. Sion, "Peacekeeping," 569.

47. Ibid.

48. Ibid., 580.

49. Ibid., 579.

50. Karim and Beardsley, "Female Peacekeepers," 469.

51. United Nations Mission in Liberia, "Gender Mainstreaming," 46.

52. Harris and Goldsmith, "Gendering Transnational Policing."

53. United Nations Peacekeeping, "Policy Dialogue," 10.

54. Harris and Goldsmith, "Gendering Transnational Policing." See also Berdahl, "Harassment Based on Sex," 647; Krimmel and Gormley, "Tokenism and Job Satisfaction," 77.

55. Rubin, "Afghan Policewomen."

56. Harris and Goldsmith, "Gendering Transnational Policing."

57. Sion, "Peacekeeping," 579.

58. Olsson, *Equal Peace.*

59. Natarajan, *Women Police.*

60. Anderholt, "Female Participation," 3809; Cordell, "Liberia Women Peacekeepers."

61. United Nations Mission in Liberia, "Gender Mainstreaming," 42.

62. Ibid.

63. Raza, "Bangladesh Police in Haiti"; Gaestel, "Liberia."

64. Tahir-Kheli, *Shirin Tahir-Kheli;* Raza, "Bangladesh Police in Haiti."

65. United Nations Mission in Liberia, "Gender Mainstreaming," 43; Gaestel, "Liberia."

66. de Alwis, Mertus, and Sajjad, "Women and Peace Processes," 185–86.

67. Allen, "Liberia."

68. Shekhar and Lord, "Women Police," 4; Natarajan, *Women Police.*

69. Karim, "Do Gender Balancing Policies," 41.

70. Walsh, "Women's Rights."

71. Pruitt, "All-Female Police Contingents."

72. Miller and Moskos, "Humanitarians or Warrors?," 628, 629–30.

73. Ibid., 628.

74. Lopes, "Militarized Masculinity," 16.

CONCLUSION

1. Mohanty, "'Under Western Eyes,'" 505.

2. Ibid., 501.

3. Ibid., 521.

4. Roy, "Confronting Empire."

References

Alaga, Ecoma, and Emma Birikorang. "Security Sector Reform and Gender: Beyond the Paradigm of Mainstreaming." Paper presented at the Annual Meeting of the International Studies Association, Montreal, March 16–19, 2011.

Aleem, Shamim. "Women in Policing in India." *Police Studies* 12 (1989): 97–103.

Allen, Bonnie. "Liberia: Female Peacekeepers Smash Stereotypes." US Embassy, September 10, 2012. http://iipdigital.usembassy.gov/st/english/publication /2012/02/20120227163049ael0.8644155.html#axzz3Fbe7PbFQ.

All Girl Squad. Prod. Shabnam Grewal. BBC2 documentary. First aired June 21, 2007.

Allred, Keith J. "Peacekeepers and Prostitutes: How Deployed Forces Fuel the Demand for Trafficked Women and New Hope for Stopping It." *Armed Forces and Society* 33, no. 1 (2006): 5–23.

"All-Women Unit of CRPF for Liberia." *Hindu* (New Delhi), January 30, 2009.

Anderholt, Charlotte. "Female Participation in Formed Police Units: A Report on the Integration of Women in Formed Police Units of Peacekeeping Operations." US Army War College Peacekeeping and Stability Operations Institute, Carlisle Barracks, PA, 2012. www.dtic.mil/cgi-bin/GetTRDoc?AD=ADA568616.

Anderlini, Sanam Naraghi. *Women Building Peace: What They Do, Why It Matters.* Boulder, CO: Lynne Riener, 2007.

Andrade, John M. *World Police and Paramilitary Forces.* New York: Stockton Press, 1985.

Avantika, Ms., and A. K. Saxena. "A Study of Career Drivers of IPS Officer Trainees." *Indian Police Journal* 59, no. 2 (2012): 8–17.

Aziz, Nuzhat. "Keepers of Peace in a Foreign Land." *Hindustan Times,* March 1, 2008.

Banerjee, Dipankar. "India." In *Providing Peacekeepers: The Politics, Challenges, and Future of United Nations Peacekeeping Contributions,* edited by Alex J. Bellamy and Paul D. Williams, 225–44. Oxford: Oxford University Press, 2013.

Basini, H. S. A. "Gender Mainstreaming Unraveled: The Case of DDRR in Liberia." *International Interactions* 39, no. 4 (2013): 535–57.

Beardsley, Kyle, Robert Blair, Michael Gilligan, and Sabrina Karim. "Gender Balancing and Its Critics: Lab-in-the-Field Evidence from the Liberian National Police." Paper presented at the Folke Bernadotte Academy Working Group on Peacekeeping, New York University, November 22–23, 2013.

Beath, Andrew, Christia Fotini, and Ruben Enikolopov. "Empowering Women through Development Aid: Evidence from a Field Experiment in Afghanistan." *American Political Science Review* 107, no. 3 (2013): 540–57.

Bedi, Kiran. *I Dare!* Delhi: Hay House, 2011.

Beede, Benjamin R. "The Roles of Paramilitary and Militarized Police." *Journal of Political and Military Sociology* 36, no. 1 (2008): 53–63.

Berdahl, Jennifer L. "Harassment Based on Sex: Protecting Social Status in the Context of Gender Hierarchy." *Academy of Management Review* 32, no. 2 (2007): 641–58.

Bhagavathy, Sunanda, and Beulah Shekhar. "Access to Justice for Victims Approaching the All Women Police Station: A SWOT Analysis." *Indian Police Journal* 59, no. 3 (2012): 100–114.

Bhasin, Ruhi. "These CRPF Cops Juggle Career, Family with Elan." *Times of India,* March 9, 2010.

Bhavnani, Rikhil R. "Do Electoral Quotas Work after They Are Withdrawn? Evidence from a Natural Experiment in India." *American Political Science Review* 103, no. 1 (2009): 23–35.

Bowman, Dina. "Studying Up, Down, Sideways and Through: Situated Research and Policy Networks." Paper presented at the Annual Meeting of the Australian Sociological Association, December 1–4, 2009.

Bridges, Donna, and Debbie Horsfall. "Increasing Operational Effectiveness in UN Peacekeeping: Toward a Gender-Balanced Force." *Armed Forces and Society* 36, no. 1 (2009): 120–30.

Chang, Ha-Joon. "The Role of Social Policy in Economic Development: Some Theoretical Reflections and Lessons from East Asia." In *Social Policy in a Development Context,* edited by Thandika Mkandawire, 246–61. London: Palgrave, 2004.

Charlesworth, Hilary. "Not Waving but Drowning: Gender Mainstreaming and Human Rights in the United Nations." *Harvard Human Rights Journal* 18 (Spring 2005): 1–18.

Cohn, Carol, ed. *Women and Wars: Contested Histories, Uncertain Futures.* Cambridge: Polity Press, 2013.

———. "Women and Wars: Toward a Conceptual Framework." In Cohn, *Women and Wars,* 1–35.

Cohn, Carol, and Ruth Jacobson. "Women and Political Activism in the Face of War and Militarization." In Cohn, *Women and Wars,* 102–23.

Cohn, Carol, Helen Kinsella, and Sheri Gibbings. "Women, Peace and Security." *International Feminist Journal of Politics* 6, no. 1 (2004): 130–40.

"Commander of All-Female Indian Police Unit Arrives in Liberia." Press Trust of India, January 23, 2007.

Conaway, Camille Pampell. *The Role of Women in Stabilization and Reconstruction.* Washington, DC: US Institute of Peace, 2006.

Conaway, Camille Pampell, and Jolynn Shoemaker. "Women in United Nations Peace Operations: Increasing the Leadership Opportunities." Women in International Security, Georgetown University, Washington, DC, 2008. http://wiisglobal.org/wp-content/uploads/2014/01/wiis_PeaceOpsFinal1.pdf.

Connell, Raewyn W. 1995. *Masculinities.* St. Leonards: Allen and Unwin.

Cordell, Kristen. "Liberia Women Peacekeepers and Human Security." *Open Democracy,* October 8, 2009.

"CRPF's All-Women Team Heads to Liberia." *NDTV* (New Delhi), video, January 19, 2007.

Davies, Sara E. "Pursuing Women's Peace and Security, and Justice." *Australian Journal of International Affairs* 67 (2013): 540–48.

de Alwis, Malathi, Julie Mertus, and Tazreena Sajjad. "Women and Peace Processes." In Cohn, *Women and Wars,* 169–93.

DeGroot, Gerard J. "A Few Good Women: Gender Stereotypes, the Military and Peacekeeping." *International Peacekeeping* 8, no. 2 (2001): 23–39.

de la Rey, Cheryl, and Susan McKay. "Peacebuilding as a Gendered Process." *Journal of Social Issues* 6, no. 1 (2006): 141–53.

Dharmapuri, Sahana. "Just Add Women and Stir?" *Parameters* 41, no. 1 (2011): 56–70.

Dunn, Michelle. "'You Will Go Far but No Further!' The Women, Peace and Security Agenda within the Post-conflict Landscape." PhD diss., University of Queensland, forthcoming.

Durch, William J., Madeline L. England, and Fiona Mangan, with Michelle Ker. *Understanding Impact of Police, Justice and Corrections Components in UN Peace Operations.* Washington, DC: Stimson Center, 2012.

Enloe, Cynthia. *The Curious Feminist: Searching for Women in a New Age of Empire.* Berkeley: University of California Press, 2004.

———. *Seriously! Investigating Crashes and Crises As If Women Mattered.* Berkeley: University of California Press, 2013.

Flood, Michael. "Why Violence against Women and Girls Happens, and How to Prevent It: A Framework and Some Key Strategies." *Redress,* August 2007, 13–19.

Ford, Liz. "UN Passes New Resolution on Women's Role in Peace Processes: Resolution 2122 Creates Roadmap for Systematic Approach to 'Implementation of Commitments on Women, Peace and Security.'" *Guardian,* October 21, 2013.

Gaestel, Allyn. "Liberia: Female Peacekeepers Empower Women to Participate in National Security." *AllAfrica,* March 15, 2010.

Gbowee, Leymah. *Mighty Be Our Powers: How Sisterhood, Prayer, and Sex Changed a Nation at War.* New York: Beast Books, 2011.

Gender and Peacebuilding Working Group, Canadian Peacebuilding Coordinating Committee. "Fact Sheet: Resolution 1325 for Girls and Young Women." 2004. www.peacebuild.ca/upload/fact_sheet.pdf (no longer accessible).

———. "Fact Sheet: Understanding United Nations Security Council Resolution 1325." 2004. www.peacebuild.ca/upload/fact_sheet_new.pdf (no longer accessible).

Gibbings, Sheri L. "No Angry Women at the United Nations: Political Dreams and the Cultural Politics of United Nations Security Council Resolution 1325." *International Feminist Journal of Politics* 13, no. 4 (2011): 522–39.

Gizelis, Theodora-Ismene, and Louise Olsson, eds. 2015. *Gender, Peace and Security: Implementing UN Security Council Resolution 1325.* London: Routledge.

Global Action to Prevent War and Armed Conflict. "Security Council Open Debate: Implementation of Resolution 1820." August 2009. www .globalactionpw.org/wp/wp-content/uploads/1820-report2.pdf.

Goodale, Mark, and Sally Engle Merry. *The Practice of Human Rights: Tracking Law between the Global and the Local.* Cambridge: Cambridge University Press, 2007.

Gowan, Richard, and Sushant K. Singh. "India and UN Peacekeeping: The Weight of History and a Lack of Strategy." In *Shaping the Emerging World: India and the Multilateral Order,* edited by Waheguru Pal Singh Sidhu, Pratap Bhanu Mehta, and Bruce Jones, 177–96. Washington, DC: Brookings Institution, 2013.

Grabosky, Peter. "Police as International Peacekeepers." *Policing and Society* 19, no. 2 (2009): 101–5.

Greener, B. K. 2009. "UNPOL: UN Police as Peacekeepers." *Policing and Society* 19, no. 2 (2009): 106–18.

Harrington, Carol. "Resolution 1325 and Post-Cold War Feminist Politics." *International Feminist Journal of Politics* 13, no. 4 (2011): 557–75.

Harris, Vandra. 2014. "Sustainable Development Following Conflicts: The Critical Role of Security and Justice." In *Linking Local and Global Sustainability*, edited by Sukhbir Sandhu, Stephen Mckenzie, and Howard Harris, 177–92. Dordrecht, the Netherlands: Springer, 2014.

Harris, Vandra, and Andrew Goldsmith. "Gendering Transnational Policing: Experiences of Australian Women in International Policing Operations." *International Peacekeeping* 17, no. 2 (2010): 292–306.

Hautzinger, Sarah J. *Violence in the City of Women: Police and Batterers in Bahia, Brazil*. Berkeley: University of California Press, 2007.

Hays, Sharon. "Structure and Agency and the Sticky Problem of Culture." *Sociological Theory* 12 (1994): 57–72.

Henry, Marsha. "Peacexploitation? Interrogating Labor Hierarchies and Global Sisterhood among Indian and Uraguayan Female Peacekeepers." *Globalizations* 9, no. 1 (2012): 15–33.

Hudson, Heidi. "Peacekeeping Trends and Their Gender Implications for Regional Peacekeeping Forces in Africa: Progress and Challenges." In Mazurana, Raven-Roberts, and Parpart, *Gender*, 111–33.

Hudson, Natalie Florea. "En-gendering UN Peacekeeping Operations." *International Journal* 60, no. 3 (2005): 785–807.

———. "Securitizing Women's Rights and Gender Equality." *Journal of Human Rights* 8, no. 1 (2009): 53–70.

Hudson, Natalie Florea, and Anne Marie Goetz. "Too Much That Can't Be Said." *International Feminist Journal of Politics* 16, no. 2 (2014): 336–46.

"India Approves Rule Requiring One-Third of Delhi Police to Be Women." *Guardian*, March 20, 2015.

"India Seeks Greater Role for Women in UN Peacekeeping." Indo-Asian News Service, October 6, 2009.

"India to Send All-Women Peacekeeper Force to Liberia." *Daily News and Analysis*, September 15, 2006.

"Indian Female Blue Berets in Liberia Mark a Historic First." Indo-Asian News Service, January 31, 2007.

"Indian Female Police Officers Inspire Liberian Women." *New Indian Express*, November 14, 2008.

"Indian Female Police Unit Wins Praise for Gender Equality." Indo-Asian News Service, August 21, 2007.

"Indiaspeak: English Is Our 2nd Language." *Times of India* (Mumbai), March 14, 2010.

International Crisis Group. "Congo: Five Priorities for a Peacebuilding Strategy." Africa Report No. 150. Washington, DC, May 11, 2009. www.crisisgroup.org/~/media/Files/africa/central-africa/dr-congo /Congo%20Five%20Priorities%20for%20a%20Peacebuilding%20Strategy .pdf.

Isaac, Thomas, and Michael Tharakan. "Kerala: Towards a New Agenda." *Economic and Political Weekly* 30, nos. 31/32 (1995): 1993–2004.

Ivanovic, Alexandra. "Why the United Nations Needs More Female Peacekeepers." July 9, 2014. United Nations University. http://unu.edu/publications/articles/why-un-needs-more-female-peacekeepers.html.

Jacobson, Ruth. "Women 'after' Wars." In Cohn, *Women and Wars,* 215–41.

Jennings, Kathleen M. "Protecting Whom? Approaches to Sexual Exploitation and Abuse in UN Peacekeeping Operations." Fafo Foundation Report. Oslo: Allkopi, 2008. www.fafo.no/~fafo/media/com_netsukii/20078.pdf.

———. "Service, Sex and Security: Gendered Peacekeeping Economies in Liberia and the Democratic Republic of the Congo." *Security Dialogue* 45, no. 4 (2014): 313–30.

———. "Women's Participation in UN Peacekeeping Operations: Agents of change or Stranded Symbols?" NOREF Report, Norwegian Peacebuilding Resource Centre, Oslo, 2011. www.resdal.org/wps/assets/women-s-participation-in-un-pk_agents-of-change-or-stranded-symbols.pdf.

Joachim, Jutta, and Andrea Schneiker. "Changing Discourses, Changing Practices? Gender Mainstreaming and Security." *Comparative European Politics* 10, no. 5 (2012): 528–63.

Jubb, Nadine, Gloria Camacho, Almachiara D'Angelo, Gina Yáñez De la Borda, Kattya Hernández, Ivonne Macassi León, Cecília MacDowell Santos, Yamileth Molina, and Wânia Pasinato. "Regional Mapping Study of Women's Police Stations in Latin America." Centro de Planificación y Estudios Sociales (CEPLAES), Quito, Ecuador, 2008. http://citeseerx.ist.psu.edu/viewdoc/download?doi=10.1.1.558.8601&rep=rep1&type=pdf.

Kabeer, Naila, Ayesha Khan, and Naysan Adlparvar. "Afghan Values or Women's Rights? Gendered Narratives about Continuity and Change in Urban Afghanistan." Institute of Development Studies Working Paper No. 387, 2011.

Karam, Azza. "Women in War and Peace-Building: The Roads Traversed, the Challenges Ahead." *International Feminist Journal of Politics* 3, no. 1 (2001): 2–25.

Karame, Kari H. "Military Women in Peace Operations: Experiences of the Norwegian Batallion in UNIFIL 1978–98." *International Peacekeeping* 8, no. 2 (2001): 85–97.

Karim, Sabrina. "Do Gender Balancing Policies Affect Post-conflict Security Sector Perceptions? Survey Evidence from Liberia." Paper presented at the International Studies Association Conference, San Francisco, 2013.

Karim, Sabrina, and Kyle Beardsley. "Female Peacekeepers and Gender Balancing: Token Gestures or Informed Policymaking?" *International Interactions: Empirical and Theoretical Research in International Relations* 39 (2013): 461–88.

Katz, Jackson. *The Macho Paradox: Why Some Men Hurt Women and How All Men Can Help*. Chicago: Sourcebooks, 2006.

Katzenstein, Mary F. "Organizing against Violence: Strategies of the Indian Women's Movement." *Pacific Affairs* 62, no. 1 (1989): 53–71.

Keck, Margaret E., and Kathryn Sikkink. *Activists beyond Borders: Advocacy Networks in International Politics*. Ithaca, NY: Cornell University Press, 1998.

Kethineni, Sesha, and Murugesan Srinivasan. "Police Handling of Domestic Violence Cases in Tamil Nadu, India." *Journal of Contemporary Criminal Justice* 25, no. 2 (2009): 202–13.

Khosa, Aasha. "CRPF's Mahila Battalion a Hit in Liberia; The Ladies from India Have Landed in Liberia." *Business Standard* (New Delhi), March 7, 2007.

King, J. S., and Paula Theliander. "Indian Formed Police Unit Provides Humanitarian Services." *UNMIL Today* 9, no. 5 (2012): 10.

Kirshenbaum, Gayle. "In U.N. Peacekeeping, Women Are an Untapped Resource." *Ms.*, January/February 1997, 20–21.

Kishwar, Madhu. "Why I Do Not Call Myself a Feminist." *Manushi* 61 (November/December 1990): 2–8.

Krimmel, John T., and Paula E. Gormley. "Tokenism and Job Satisfaction for Policewomen." *American Journal of Criminal Justice* 28, no. 1 (2003): 73–88.

Krishnasamy, Kabilan. "A Case for India's 'Leadership' in United Nations Peacekeeping." *International Studies* 47, nos. 2–4 (2012): 225–46.

Kronsell, Annica. "Methods for Studying Silences: Gender Analysis in Institutions of Hegemonic Masculinity." In *Feminist Methodologies in International Relations*, edited by B. Brooke Ackerly, Maria Stern, and Jacqui True, 108–28. Cambridge: Cambridge University Press, 2006.

Liebowitz, Debra J., and Susanne Zwingel. "Gender Equality Oversimplified: Using CEDAW to Counter the Measurement Obsession." *International Studies Review* 16 (2014): 362–89.

Lopes, Hayley. "Militarized Masculinity in Peacekeeping Operations: An Obstacle to Gender Mainstreaming." Background paper, Peacebuild/Paix Durable, Ottawa, 2011. http://peacebuild.ca/Lopes%20website%20ready.pdf.

MacKenzie, Megan H. *Female Soldiers in Sierra Leone*. New York: NYU Press, 2012.

March, James G., and Johan Olsen. "The Institutional Dynamics of International Political Orders." *International Organization* 52, no. 4 (1998): 943–69.

Mathers, Jennifer G. "Women and State Military Forces." In Cohn, *Women and Wars*, 125–45.

Mazurana, Dyan. "Do Women Matter in Peacekeeping? Women in Police, Military and Civilian Peacekeeping." *Canadian Women's Studies* 22, no. 2 (2002): 23–38.

———. "Women, Girls, and Non-state Armed Opposition Groups." In Cohn, *Women and Wars*, 146–68.

Mazurana, Dyan, Angela Raven-Roberts, and Jane Parpart, eds. *Gender, Conflict, and Peacekeeping*. Lanham, MD: Rowman and Littlefield, 2005.

Mazurana, Dyan, Angela Raven-Roberts, and Jane Parpart, with Sue Lautze. Introduction to Mazurana, Raven-Roberts, and Parpart, *Gender*, 1–26.

Meger, Sara. "Toward a Feminist Political Economy of Wartime Sexual Violence: The Case of the Democratic Republic of Congo." *International Feminist Journal of Politics* 17, no. 3 (2014). DOI: 10.1080/14616742.2014.941253.

Meier, Kenneth J., and Jill Nicholson-Crotty. "Gender, Representative Bureaucracy, and Law Enforcement: The Case of Sexual Assault." *Public Administration Review* 66, no. 6 (2006): 850–60.

Merry, Sally Engle. "Rights Talk and the Experience of Law: Implementing Women's Human Rights to Protection from Violence." *Human Rights Quarterly* 25, no. 2 (2003): 343–81.

Miller, Laura L., and Charles Moskos. "Humanitarians or Warrors? Race, Gender, and Combat Status in Operation Restore Hope." *Armed Forces and Society* 21, no. 4 (1995): 615–37.

Mohanty, Chandra T. "'Under Western Eyes' Revisited: Feminist Solidarity through Anticapitalist Struggles." *Signs: Journal of Women in Culture and Society* 28, no. 2 (2002): 499–535.

Nader, Laura. "Key Note Address." Presented at the Fifth Annual Public Anthropology Conference: Supporting Social Movements, American University, Washington, DC, October 31–November 1, 2008.

———. "Up the Anthropologist: Perspectives Gained from 'Studying Up.'" In *Reinventing Anthropology*, edited by Dell H. Hymes, 284–311. New York: Random House, 1969.

Narayan, Uma. "Cross-cultural Connections, Border-Crossings, and 'Death by Culture': Thinking about Dowry-Murders in India and Domestic-Violence Murders in the United States." In *Theorizing Feminisms: A Reader*, edited by Elizabeth Hackett and Sally Haslanger, 62–78. Oxford: Oxford University Press, 2006.

Natarajan, Mangai. *Women Police in a Changing Society*. Farnham, UK: Ashgate, 2008.

———. "Women Police Units in India: A New Direction." *Police Studies* 19, no. 2 (1996): 63–76.

Naughtie, James. "Liberia: Rape and Sexual Violence 'Endemic.'" *BBC News Africa*, April 10, 2013.

"New Mandates Boosted the Success of UN Peacekeeping: Mehta." Press Trust of India, June 1, 2007.

Ofori, Rosaline. "Call to Enhance Women's Leadership in Regional Peace and Security." *UNMIL Today* 9, no. 5 (2012): 1.

Olsson, Louise. *Equal Peace: United Nations Peace Operations and the Power-Relations between Men and Women in Timor-Leste.* Department of Peace and Conflict Research Report Series. Uppsala: University of Uppsala, Department of Peace and Conflict Research, 2007.

———. "The Namibian Peace Operation in a Gender Context." In Mazurana, Raven-Roberts, and Parpart, *Gender,* 168–82.

Olsson, Louise, and Theodora-Ismene Gizelis. "An Introduction to Resolution 1325: Measuring Progress and Impact." In Olsson and Gizelis, *Gender,* 1–15.

Olsson, Louise, Anita Schjølset, and Frida Möller. "Women's Participation in International Operations and Missions." In Olsson and Gizelis, *Gender,* 37–61.

Ospina, Sofi. *Ten-Year Impact Study on Implementation of UN Security Council Resolution 1325 (2000) on Women, Peace and Security in Peacekeeping: Final Report to the United Nations Department of Peacekeeping Operations, Department of Field Support.* New York: United Nations, 2010.

Pankhurst, Donna. "The 'Sex War' and Other Wars: Towards a Feminist Approach to Peace Building." *Development in Practice* 13, no. 2 (2003): 154–77.

Paris, Roland. "Peacekeeping and the Constraints of Global Culture." *European Journal of International Relations* 9, no. 3 (2003): 441–73.

Poole, Avery Dorothy Howard. "Institutional Change in Regional Organizations: The Emergence and Evolution of ASEAN Norms." PhD diss., University of British Columbia, 2013.

———. "'The World Is Outraged': Legitimacy in the Making of the ASEAN Human Rights Body." Lecture presented at the Centre for Public Policy, University of Melbourne.

Porter, Elisabeth. "Women, Political Decision-Making, and Peace-Building." *Global Change, Peace and Security* 15, no. 3 (2003): 245–62.

Pruitt, Lesley J. "All-Female Police Contingents: Feminism and the Discourse of Armed Protection." *International Peacekeeping* 20, no. 1 (2013): 67–79.

———. "Looking Back, Moving Forward: The Role of the International Community in Addressing Conflict-Related Sexual Violence." *Journal of Women, Politics and Policy* 33, no. 4 (2012): 299–321.

Pupavac, Vanessa. "Empowering Women? An Assessment of International Gender Policies in Bosnia." *International Peacekeeping* 12, no. 3 (2005): 391–405.

"RAF Deploys Women for UN Operation." *Times of India,* October 8, 2006.

Rankin, Katharine N. "Governing Development: Neoliberalism, Microcredit, and Rational Economic Woman." *Economy and Society* 30, no. 1 (2001): 18–37.

Raven-Roberts, Angela. "Gender Mainstreaming in United Nations Peacekeeping Operations: Talking the Talk, Tripping over the Walk." In Mazurana, Raven-Roberts, and Parpart, *Gender,* 43–64.

———. "Women and the Political Economy of War." In Cohn, *Women and Wars,* 36–53.

Raza, Razzak. "Bangladesh Police in Haiti." *Blitz,* May 26, 2010.

Rehn, Elisabeth, and Ellen Johnson Sirleaf. *Women, War and Peace: The Independent Experts' Assessment of the Impact of Armed Conflict on Women and Women's Roles in Peace-Building.* New York: UNIFEM, 2002. www .unfpa.org/sites/default/files/pub-pdf/3F71081FF391653DC1256C690031 70E9-unicef-WomenWarPeace.pdf.

Roy, Arundhati. "Confronting Empire." Paper presented at World Social Forum, Porto Allegre, 2003.

Rubin, Alissa J. "Afghan Policewomen Say Sexual Harassment Is Rife." *New York Times,* September 16, 2013.

Rubinstein, Robert A. "Methodological Challenges in the Ethnographic Study of Multilateral Peacekeeping." *PoLAR: Political and Legal Anthropology Review* 21, no. 1 (1999): 138–49.

———. *Peacekeeping under Fire: Culture and Intervention.* Boulder, CO: Paradigm, 2008.

Schäfer, Rita. *Masculinity and Civil Wars in Africa: New Approaches to Overcoming Sexual Violence in War.* Federal Ministry for Economic Cooperation and Development: Program Promoting Gender Equality and Women's Rights. Eschborn: Deutsche Gesellschaft für Technische Zusammenarbeit, 2009.

Schjølset, Anita. *NATO and the Women: Exploring the Gender Gap in the Armed Forces.* PRIO Papers. Oslo: Peace Research Institute Oslo, 2010.

Segal, Mady W. "Women's Military Roles Cross-nationally: Past, Present, and Future." *Gender and Society* 9, no. 6 (1995): 757–75.

Sharma, Aman. "UN Showers Praise on CRPF Women's Unit in Liberia." *Mail Today* (New Delhi), August 16, 2010.

Sharma, Betwa. 2009. "Indian Women Peacekeepers an Inspiration for Liberians." Press Trust of India, November 21, 2009.

Shekhar, Beulah, and Vivian B. Lord. "Women Police in Southern India: Aftermath of New Delhi Gang Rape." *Police Forum* 22 (2013): 4–10.

Shepherd, Laura J. "Sex, Security and Superhero(in)es: From 1325 to 1820 and Beyond." *International Feminist Journal of Politics* 13, no. 4 (2011): 504–21.

Shourie, Dharam. "First All-Women UN Peacekeeping Unit Takes Charge in Liberia." Press Trust of India, January 31, 2007.

Siebold, Guy L. "Core Issues and Theory in Military Sociology." *Journal of Political and Military Sociology* 29, no. 1 (2001): 140–59.

Simić, Olivera. "Does the Presence of Women Really Matter? Towards Combating Male Sexual Violence in Peacekeeping Operations." *International Peacekeeping* 17, no. 2 (2010): 188–99.

Singhal, Rekha. "Women, Gender and Development: The Evolution of Theories and Practice." *Psychology and Developing Societies* 15 (2003): 165–85.

Sion, Liora. 2008. "Peacekeeping and the Gender Regime." *Journal of Contemporary Ethnography* 37, no. 5 (2008): 561–85.

Sirleaf, Ellen Johonson. *Speech by Ellen Johnson-Sirleaf at the WIP Annual Summit 2013*. Speech presented at Summit of Women in Parliament Global Forum, Brussels, November 27, 2013. YouTube video, uploaded December 4, 2013.

———. *This Child Will Be Great: Memoir of a Remarkable Life by Africa's First Woman President*. New York: Harper Perennial, 2009.

Sjoberg, Laura. *Gender, War, and Conflict*. Cambridge: Polity Press, 2014.

Skjelsbaek, Inger. "Sexual Violence in Times of War: A New Challenge for Peace Operations?" *International Peacekeeping* 8, no. 2 (2007): 69–84.

Steinberg, Donald. "Beyond Victimhood: Engaging Women in the Pursuit of Peace." Testimony to the House of Representatives Committee on Foreign Affairs, Subcommittee on International Organizations, Human Rights and Oversight, May 15, 2008.

Stiehm, Judith H. "Women, Peacekeeping and Peacemaking: Gender Balance and Mainstreaming." *International Peacekeeping* 8, no. 2 (2001): 39–49.

Tahir-Kheli, Shirin. *Shirin Tahir-Kheli on Female Peacekeeping Forces*. Video interview by Better World Campaign, 2008. UN Foundation. www.unfoundation.org/news-and-media/multimedia/videocasts/shirin-tahir-kheli-on-female-1.html.

Thakur, Ramesh. "Unintended Consequences of Blue Berets' Actions." *Hindu* (New Delhi), May 25, 2007.

"Tharoor on a Six-Day Visit to Liberia, Ghana." Indo-Asian News Service, September 16, 2009.

Theidon, Kimberly, and Kelly Phenicie, with Elizabeth Murray. *Gender, Conflict, and Peacebuilding: State of the Field and Lessons Learned from USIP Grantworking*. Washington, DC: United States Institute of Peace, 2011.

Tickner, J. Ann. *A Feminist Voyage through International Relations*. Oxford: Oxford University Press, 2014.

True, Jacqui. *The Political Economy of Violence against Women*. Oxford: Oxford University Press, 2012.

True, Jacqui, and Michael Mintrom. "Transnational Networks and Policy Diffusion: The Case of Gender Mainstreaming." *International Studies Quarterly* 45 (2001): 27–57.

Tryggestad, Torunn L. "The UN Peacebuilding Commission and Gender: A Case of Norm Reinforcement." *International Peacekeeping* 17, no. 2 (2010): 159–71.

"UN Envoy Welcomes New Batch of Indian Policewomen to Liberia." United News of India, February 9, 2008.

"UNGA President Praises Indian Women's Contingent in Liberia." Press Trust of India, May 30, 2007.

United Nations Department of Peacekeeping Operations. *Background Note: United Nations Peacekeeping.* New York: United Nations Department of Public Information, 2011. www.un.org/en/peacekeeping/documents /backgroundnote.pdf.

———. "WANTED Skilled Police Officers REWARD: Peace and Security." *UN Police Magazine,* 2012.

United Nations Department of Political Affairs et al. "Conflict Related Sexual Violence and Peace Negotiations: Implementing Security Council Resolution 1820. Report on the High-Level Colloquium Organized by DPA, DPKO, OCHA, UNDP and UNIFEM on Behalf of New York, UN Action against Sexual Violence in Conflict, and in Partnership with the Centre for Humanitarian Dialogue." June 22–23, 2009. www.hdcentre.org/fileadmin/user _upload/Our_work/Mediation_support/Current%20activities/1%20 Gender%20and%20Mediation/Gender%20main%20page/Supporting _documents/JuneColloquium-SummaryReport.pdf.

United Nations Department of Public Information."Female Police Keep the Peace in Liberia." News release, 2007 (no exact date). www.un.org/works /sub3.asp?lang=en&id=51 (no longer accessible).

United Nations Mission in Liberia. "Gender Mainstreaming in Peacekeeping Operations Liberia, 2003–2009: Best Practices Report." September 2010. www.resdal.org/facebook/UNMIL_Gender_Mainstreaming_in_PKO_in _Liberia-Best.pdf.

United Nations News Centre. "UN Peacekeeping: On the Front Lines to End Violence against Women." News release, March 8, 2013. www.un.org/apps /news/story.asp?NewsID=44325#.VobvbTa4mqQ.

United Nations Peacekeeping. "Fact Sheet: United Nations Peacekeeping." March 2010. www.un.org/en/peacekeeping/documents/factsheet.pdf.

———. "Gender Statistics by Mission for the Month of April 2015." May 6, 2015. www.un.org/en/peacekeeping/contributors/gender/2015gender /apr15.pdf.

———. "Policy Dialogue to Review Strategies For Enhancing Gender Balance among Uniformed Personnel in Peacekeeping Missions: Final Report." United Nations, New York, March 28–29, 2006. www.un.org/womenwatch /ianwge/taskforces/wps/Final%20Report%20TCC%20PCC%20Policy%20 Dialouge%20_English_.pdf.

———. "Women in Peacekeeping." n.d. Retrieved January 5, 2012. www.un.org /en/peacekeeping/issues/women/womeninpk.shtml.

United Nations Security Council. Resolution 1820, S/RES/1820 (2008).

———. "Women, Peace and Security: Sexual Violence in Conflict and Sanctions." Security Council Report No. 2. April 10, 2013. www.securitycouncilreport .org/atf/cf/%7B65BFCF9B-6D27-4E9C-8CD3-CF6E4FF96FF9%7D/cross _cutting_report_2_women_peace_security_2013.pdf.

"UN Seeks More Female Peacekeepers." UNI (United News of India), June 11, 2010.

Vlachova, Marie, and Lea Biason. *Women in an Insecure World: Violence against Women Facts, Figures and Analysis.* Geneva: Geneva Centre for the Democratic Control of Armed Forces, 2005.

Walker, Margaret Urban. *Moral Understandings: A Feminist Study in Ethics.* Oxford: Oxford University Press, 2007.

Walsh, Shannon Drysdale. "Engendering Justice: Constructing Institutions to Address Violence against Women." *Studies in Social Justice* 2 (2008): 48–62.

———. "Women's Rights as Human Rights in Latin America: State Response to Violence against Women." Paper presented at the Annual Meeting of the International Studies Association, Montreal, 2011.

Whitworth, Sandra. 2004. *Men, Militarism, and UN Peacekeeping: A Gendered Analysis.* Boulder, CO: Lynne Rienner, 2004.

"The Woman Who Took on Zimbabwe's Security Men and Won." *African Dream* series, BBC, July 6, 2012. www.bbc.com/news/world-africa-17896466.

"Women on Top in Peace Force." *Hindustan Times,* June 6, 2006.

"Women UN Peacekeepers—More Needed." IRIN: Humanitarian News and Analysis, May 20, 2010. www.irinnews.org/report/89194/.

Woolsey, Shannon. "Challenges for Women in Policing." *Law and Order* 58, no. 10 (2010): 78–80, 82.

Young, Holly. "Women on the Beat: How to Get More Female Police Officers around the World." *Guardian,* July 28, 2015.

Index

activism, 5, 29, 120, 121

Adlparvar, Naysan, 69

all-female formed police unit (FFPU): assisting victims, 2, 12, 32, 33, 59–61, 64, 101–2; gender mainstreaming, 89–90, 93, 96–99, 114, 116–118; recruitment, 28, 40–42, 56, 61, 70, 80–82, 112; second shift (community work expectation), 12–13, 42, 52, 72–74, 79, 81, 83, 117–18, 135n48; training, 1, 12, 38–40–47, 54–56, 60–64, 70, 80, 91–93, 112, 118; Women, Peace, and Security agenda, 9, 17, 21, 27, 67, 116–117, 119. *See also* all-women police station; Central Reserve Police Force; Department of Peacekeeping Operations (DPKO), United Nations; formed police unit (FPU) (gender non-specific); gender mainstreaming; Mahila Battalion; marginalization of women; participation of women; role models

all-female policies, 89–90. *See also* policy

all-female spaces, 2, 8, 89–90, 120

All Girl Squad (BBC documentary film), 21, 75

all-women police station (AWPS), 30–34, 40, 48, 130n29. *See also* all-female formed police unit (FFPU)

all-women police units (AWPU), 32. *See also* all-female formed police unit (FFPU)

American Heritage Dictionary, 5

Anderholt, Charlotte, 78, 98, 104

appropriateness, 9, 12, 41, 64, 86, 89, 92, 93, 96–101, 118. *See also* global culture; male predominance

Arnado, Mary Anne, 92

Australia, gender-integration, 89

AWPS. *See* all-women police station

AWPU (all-women police unit), 32. *See also* all-female formed police unit (FFPU)

Banerjee, Dipankar, 39, 129n1

Bangladesh, 1, 36, 113, 120

Beardsley, Kyle, 63

Bedi, Kiran, 11, 27, 37–40, 48, 105–6

bias. *See* gender bias

Biason, Lea, 102

Birikorang, Emma, 104

blue helmets, 35

blue tape, 35, 103, 107. *See also* participation of women: barriers

boys: "boys will be boys" attitude, 7, 109; participation in violence, 12, 17, 63; school attendance, 81. *See also* gendered violence; masculinity